LIFT YOUR HEARTS ON HIGH

Eucharistic Prayer in the Reformed Tradition

Ronald P. Byars

WESTMINSTER
JOHN KNOX PRESS
LOUISVILLE • KENTUCKY

Book design by Sharon Adams
Cover design by Night and Day Design
Cover photographs: Photodisc Green and Comstock/Getty Images:

First edition
Published by Westminster John Knox Press
Louisville, Kentucky

This book is printed on acid-free paper that meets the American National Standards Institute Z39.48 standard. ∞

PRINTED IN THE UNITED STATES OF AMERICA

05 06 07 08 09 10 11 12 13 14 — 10 9 8 7 6 5 4 3 2 1

Library of Congress Cataloging-in-Publication Data

Byars, Ronald P.
    Lift your hearts on high : Eucharistic prayer in the Reformed tradition / Ronald P. Byars.
        p. cm.
    Includes bibliographical references and index.
    ISBN 0-664-22855-0 (alk. paper)
    1. Eucharistic prayers. 2. Catholic Church—Doctrines. 3. Protestant churches—Doctrines. I. Title.

    BV825.54B92 2005
    264'.04036—dc22

                                                                    2005042220

In thanksgiving for Pres and Ione Byars,
John and Grace Rhodes

Contents

Acknowledgments

This book originated with my inaugural lecture as Professor of Preaching and Worship at Union Theological Seminary and Presbyterian School of Christian Education (Union PSCE) on May 9, 2001. Parts of it were later published in *Worship* 77 (March 2003).

I owe a debt of thanks to President Louis Weeks; the dean of the theology faculty, John Carroll; and to my students and faculty colleagues, particularly the members of the Department of Practical Theology on the Richmond campus: Beverly Zink-Sawyer, Kurtis Hess, Syngman Rhee, Charles Brown, Carol Schweitzer, Ken McFayden, and Jane Vann, for their friendship and for the opportunity to serve alongside them. Thanks to Dean James Brashler, who helped me understand some Dutch texts as I worked on this project, and to Professor Brian Gerrish, who read and offered helpful comments on chapter 3.

I am grateful as well for the continual support of my wife, Susan Rhodes Byars, who has supported my vocation as though it were her own, often at sacrifice to her own interests. Our sons, Stephen and Matthew, have married wisely, and I am grateful to them and to Lisa Blackadar and Melissa Byars for the joy they bring to my life and work, and for the gifts of Jonas, Audrey, Grace, and Benjamin Byars.

David Dobson, first senior editor and now director of product management at the Presbyterian Publishing Corporation, has been helpful and encouraging. Julie Tonini and others at Presbyterian Publishing have brought special care and expertise to preparing the manuscript for publication. My thanks to Donald K. McKim, who served as editor for this book.

The congregations of the Allen Park Presbyterian Church, Allen Park, Michigan (and especially its longtime pastor, the late Dr. Wanzer H. Brunelle); the Presbyterian Church of Okemos, Michigan; Second Presbyterian Church, Lexington, Kentucky; and First Presbyterian Church, Birmingham, Michigan, have contributed enormously to my teaching and scholarship. I am grateful to them and to my colleagues in the Presbytery of Detroit. Thanks also to the people and staff of Second Presbyterian Church, Richmond, Virginia, for the pleasure of sharing the life of that congregation.

Ronald P. Byars
Richmond, Virginia
August 12, 2004

Introduction

Garrison Keillor tells the story of a young family en route to Lake Wobegon for Thanksgiving. The father was driving, his wife beside him, and their two children rode in the back seat. They would be spending Thanksgiving with Dad's parents. About halfway to Lake Wobegon, it occurred to Dad that his own father would certainly say grace before the meal. He and his wife had been raised in the church, but hadn't been to worship for years. He hurriedly began to orient his children. He told them that before dinner, they would all bow their heads while Grandfather thanked God for the food. From the back seat his daughter asked, curiously, "Who's God?"

Certainly the child's question is one that might well be asked by a good many other children whose grandparents practice the Christian faith, but whose own parents, whether or not they choose to identify themselves as Christians, no longer practice it even in the simplest ways. In childhood, these parents acquired some acquaintance with the biblical stories and perhaps a rudimentary theology, but they no longer attend public worship, or teach bedtime prayers to their children, or pray before meals. Their own children, experiencing no formation in the faith, will inherit not even the barest sense of Christian identity. Thus the question that may startle even the nonpracticing parent, "Who's God?" How does the church answer that query?

A similar question that surfaces in an increasingly pluralistic culture might be, "Whose God?" Since 9/11, Americans have discovered the Muslims among us. In years past, I used to take members of church youth groups to visit a local mosque or Islamic center. Typically the prayer leader or imam would try to explain who Muslims were and what Islam is about. Using the method of teaching by contrast, the spokesperson would often begin by contrasting the Muslim belief in the oneness of God with Christian belief in the Holy Trinity. Clearly, Muslim and Christian ways of speaking about God are similar, and yet dramatically different. If one aspect of Christian worship is that the holy God may become manifest in the worshipping assembly, how should our worship render the character and disposition of a God whom Christians know as one-in-three, three-in-one?

A TRINITARIAN GOD

From as early as the New Testament era, the evidence seems to be that Christian worship on the Lord's Day included both Word (Scriptures read and proclaimed) and Sacrament (the Lord's Supper). Each in its own way exhibited the character and disposition of the God worshipped in those early Christian assemblies. While Scriptures read aloud and proclaimed used words, stories, and verbal images as well as reasoned discourse to set before the assembly the God revealed in Jesus Christ, the Lord's Supper set the same God before the assembly in both words and actions. With ear and eye, taste, touch, and smell, those who gathered around Word and Table could come to discern directly and indirectly both who God is and whose God was being served in that place.

Not long ago, I attended services in a congregation whose newspaper ad had identified it as "Christ-centered." Certainly that seemed a good thing, except that I remembered Richard Niebuhr's caution that there is more than one way of being unitarian, and that a good many Christians were, perhaps unwittingly, unitarians of the second person. Very often, Protestant worship has muted the Trinitarian character of God. It may be muted in the interest of being "Christ-centered," or in some cases, "Spirit-centered," or even "creation-centered." Sometimes it may be muted because the traditional language of Father-Son-Spirit cannot easily be modified with integrity, and the male references embarrass us. Or the doctrine of the Trinity may be so difficult that ministers hesitate to puzzle or even antagonize congregations who prefer their Christianity made inoffensively simple. Perhaps it may even be the case that some think of the Trinity as an esoteric add-on, of interest only in the seminary, with no important consequences for faith, worship, or life in the world.

The word "God" is used widely in our culture and often indiscriminately. It may serve as only the vaguest of references to some anonymous higher power or hidden hand that governs the universe. When devout Hindus use the word, with or without a capital G, they understand it in a way that runs from somewhat similar to radically different from what Muslims mean when they refer to Allah. As used by Christian Scientists or Mormons, the same word hides quite different perceptions of the divine being, different both from each other and from Christians in the historic churches. To discover the subtleties of the various renderings of the divine, one may read books or consult experts on religious doctrine, or one may observe whether the people using the word "God" pray and, if they do, whether they pray together and, if so, how.

Whose God is portrayed in Friday prayers at the mosque? Whose God is portrayed in the chants at the Hare Krishna temple? And who is the God named in the public worship of the Christian church? From early centuries, answers to the questions "Whose God?" and "Who's God?" could be discovered in the eucharistic prayer of the church—the table graces offered each Lord's Day in the Christian assembly.

THE IDENTITY AND CHARACTER OF GOD

In offering this book, my intent is to say that eucharistic prayer—often called the Great Thanksgiving—is a subject of interest not only to liturgical scholars. The way we pray at the Holy Table acquaints the worshipping congregation with the God of Genesis, the exodus, and Sinai, who is also the God of Jesus Christ and the God of Pentecost, whom Christian faith understands in ways both similar to and different from the several ways our Muslim, Hindu, Christian Science, Mormon, or secular neighbors use the same three-letter word. Our prayer at Table acquaints us with the God who is Holy Trinity, and does so not only cognitively, but also subliminally, as our unconscious absorbs the meaning of words, actions, gestures, and records them in the heart as well as the mind.

Church leaders who long to form congregations whose faith runs deep enough that they can and will choose to love and serve the God of Scripture and church, even when many other attractive choices are available, will discover that liturgical prayer—and particularly the Great Thanksgiving—may serve as a strong asset in their armory.

This book means to offer the reader a fuller appreciation of the Great Prayer, based on a deeper acquaintance with its links to Jewish prayer; with its historical development in the early centuries of the Christian era; and with its ecumenical roots; as well as with issues that emerged before, during, and after the Reformation of the sixteenth century. It will advocate attentiveness to eucharistic prayer not only as a positive affirmation of the essential unity of the church, but also as a means of nurturing congregations in the Trinitarian faith that, typically and at our peril, we take for granted, but that is essential for the formation of an authentically Christian identity in a time of religious crisis.

SECULAR, BUT EXTRAVAGANTLY RELIGIOUS

We live in a time that is remarkably secular, while at the same time extravagantly but indifferently religious. For the church to be faithful to its calling, it matters in which God we trust and believe. The Eucharist, grounded in eucharistic praying, draws us to the God revealed to prophets and apostles and to the women and men of the historic church, who together compose the great communion of saints witnessing to this God who is at one and the same time Father, Son, and Holy Spirit.

Some Presbyterians and other Protestants have understood their tradition to be one that has no use for ritual. There is, of course, a certain amount of historical amnesia at work here, since both John Calvin and John Knox, not to mention the English Puritans and John Wesley, produced liturgical texts and forms intended to serve as norms for public worship. The past few centuries have not been hospitable to ritual—at least, to ritual that is unapologetically itself. The rationalism that is one of the fruits of the Enlightenment has so thoroughly shaped the worldview of Protestants that we imagine that ritual is nothing but a crutch for the intellectually weak, and naively, that we have succeeded in creating worship without ritual. Our reverence for the sermon has often obscured the fact that preaching itself is a form of ritual.

Every religious body has rituals, whether recognized as such or not. Even the silent meetings of the Society of Friends have a ritual form, as will be obvious to anyone attending such a meeting for the first time, who will undoubtedly experience the uncertainty common to all who visit a worshipping assembly without knowing quite what to do. Those who surf the cable television community-access channels will find that even the churches that most vociferously condemn "ritual" follow their own rites. They may not be written down, but the same phrases appear in prayer over and over, and the same actions follow in rather predictable sequence from week to week. Even the so-called "seeker services" and their near kin, the "contemporary service," are quite predictable after the first experience. There is no religious assembly without ritual. Any group that meets more than once is bound to repeat itself. The real issue is not whether or not to employ ritual in worship, but which ritual.

ARE THERE LITURGICAL NORMS?

Ironically, the very disdain for traditional ritual that has proven such an attractive feature of Protestantism since the Enlightenment is no longer so attractive in the emerging postmodern culture. We are witnessing among younger generations a renaissance of longing for worship that is experiential as well as rational. For many, this yearning leads to Pentecostalism. For others, it has led beyond the Christian church to experimentation with various forms of New Age spirituality. For many others, it is leading to a new openness to ritual in specifically Christian forms. What the Enlightenment culture considered uncouth and obsolete appears to many in the postmodern culture to be a way of knowing and relating to God equal to and complementary to cognitive ways of knowing. For such a time as this, the church may reclaim Sacrament alongside Word.

Presbyterians are accustomed to affirming doctrinal norms, as represented by the various Reformed confessions, but we have been less accustomed to thinking in terms of liturgical norms, even though we have a long history of according constitutional status to at least a minimum of liturgical norms, as represented by the various Directories for Worship, beginning with the first Westminster Directory in 1644. Perhaps one reason for this is that, as a church originating in the Reformation, our historical memory is one of dissenting from the sixteenth-century norm as represented by the medieval Catholic church. In Presbyterian consciousness, there seems to be an almost instinctive need to distance ourselves from Roman Catholic practice, frequently without much discrimination. If the Catholics do something, then our obligation is not to do it, or to do exactly the opposite. (Of course, Roman Catholic practice has frequently been shaped by exactly the same desire to distinguish themselves from Protestants!)

OLD ADVERSARIES MAY BE NEW ALLIES

The time in which the world of Europe and North America divided itself into a choice between Protestant and Catholic is long gone. Not only do we live with enormous religious diversity, including growing numbers of Muslims, Hindus, and Buddhists among us; but the process of reform within the Roman Catholic Church, beginning with Vatican Council II, has permanently altered the nature of the relationship between Protestants and Catholics. In North America and Europe in the twenty-first century, Protestants (at least, the historic churches) and Roman Catholics continue to have serious differences, but viewed within the context of the larger society, each has reason to see the other as basically on the same side as we discover how to be the church in a religiously plural society, a secular society, and a society in which many Christians, of whatever background, have minimal acquaintance with the great matters of the faith.

If the historically adversarial relationship between the churches of the Reformation and the Roman Catholic Church has been remarkably transformed in the past half century, then perhaps this is a time in which Presbyterians can see without prejudice what has always been true: that the Reformed tradition, of which Presbyterians are a part, is first of all a movement within the catholic church, and not a movement out of it. Calvin, who read, studied, and quoted the church fathers, had no notion of creating a new church but, rather, was trying to reform the existing church. He did not understand the Reformed movement to be leaping back over sixteen centuries to start the church all over again, as though one could pick up where the New Testament generations left off. Protestants we are, but nevertheless there is a history and tradition with which we have to do. We may affirm that history and tradition, or critique it, or even denounce it, but we are accountable to it.

Everything that happened between the end of the New Testament era and Calvin's own day belongs to the folk who rallied around the Reformed banner as much as to those who were determined to resist their reforms. The ancient wisdom of the desert fathers and mothers; the contributions of monastic communities and pre-Reformation theologians, musicians, and hymn writers both East and West; the things worthy of praise and the things worthy of condemnation all belong equally to the Reformed as to Catholic or Orthodox. Francis of Assisi and the Inquisition are both, for good or ill, "ours" and not just "theirs."

SOMETIMES WHAT'S NEW IS WHAT'S OLD

While Calvin and other reformers certainly did break with many medieval doctrines and practices, they did so within the specific context of their situation in the sixteenth century. With reference to eucharistic prayer in particular, they broke with the practice of the priest reciting nearly all of the prayer sotto voce in a foreign language, and with the fact that the prayer only rarely reached its consummation in the communion of the people. These and other "deformations" of the Eucharist have been corrected in the twentieth century by actions of the Second Vatican Council.

In an increasingly fragmented Protestantism, it behooves the historic churches to play a conservative role with respect to the broad ecumenical tradition of the whole church, both West and East. I mean "conservative" not in an ideological sense, but in the sense of not discarding too quickly those norms that have provided a center of gravity—a center that can help spare the church from the sectarian disintegration that occurs when those norms have been forgotten or discarded. Roman Catholic "conservatism" at the Second Vatican Council took the form not of resisting change, but of reexamining current eucharistic prayer and practice in favor of a return to norms that preceded medieval developments; the historic Protestant churches might be so bold as to follow their example.

In fact, Protestant churches have been following their example, albeit more slowly and by fits and starts. A remarkable consensus of scholarship occurred in the twentieth century, during which biblical, historical, and theological studies have led to a sort of convergence of Christian traditions that have long stood apart. One example of that consensus is represented by the World Council of Churches document, *Baptism, Eucharist and Ministry*.[1]

Liturgical change among Presbyterians and other Protestants, unlike change for Roman Catholics, requires winning the confidence and consent of pastors, church officers, and church members. Denominations have produced service books that reflect the twentieth-century consensus and even made changes in official liturgical directories. The hardest step is to get the attention of those responsible for actually implementing changes. And why should they?

It's not a matter of the third, fourth, and fifth centuries being a kind of golden age to which all are obligated to return, but that much evidence points to that period's vigorous liturgical life, in which the whole congregation played an active role and in which both Word and Sacrament carried great weight. It is this—active participation, and the renewal of both Word and Sacrament— that serves as a model for the historic churches. Historical study shows that the church of the early centuries took very seriously the role of the liturgy, including eucharistic prayer, in both expressing a consensus theology and helping to form the faith of the people of God in ways that were biblically and theologically sound.

In a time when independent churches spring up in every suburb, quite typically indifferent to the ongoing conversation that has helped to shape the faith of the church since New Testament times, and in which novelty is very often the prevailing value, the historic churches need to identify their allies. Are their allies the nondenominational congregations whose doctrine and worship are shaped primarily and idiosyncratically by their pastors? Or are our allies those whose long history, much of it shared with us, has given them credentials to be heard among us? I would argue that, while Presbyterians and others might learn a good deal from the independent ecclesiastical start-ups, our truest allies are the other churches of the Reformation and the Roman Catholic and Orthodox churches from which they sprang.

REFORMED AND ECUMENICAL

In this book I will attempt to look specifically at eucharistic prayer from that point of view. It should not be a strange perspective, since the current PCUSA Directory for Worship, which has constitutional authority among us,

describes eucharistic prayer in terms of historic norms, both Reformed and
ecumenical. I am a Presbyterian and write within a Presbyterian historical,
theological, and contemporary perspective. However, since the Presbyterian
experience is quite typical of the experience of other Protestants, and Presbyterians have understood themselves from their origins to be ecumenical, this
book will be useful to other Christians as well. My appeal, however, is
addressed particularly to my denominational kindred, for whom I feel a special responsibility and who, I sincerely hope, will lead the way, in these days of
"worship wars," to the renewal of sacramental life to stand alongside their
long-held commitment to the ministry of the Word.

Who is God? And whose God is the One around whom the Christian
church gathers? These are the questions with which the church struggled in
its first centuries, when it was a minority in an alien culture. The church struggled with such questions not only in formal theological debate, but in the formation of its liturgical life. Eucharistic prayer, as it took shape from the New
Testament period on, implicitly offers a reply to those questions, which are as
crucial to us in our time as they were to Christians of those times.

That reply, as it developed and as we receive it, is that the God who has
called and gathered us is Holy Trinity: at one and the same time Father, Son,
and Holy Spirit. The Trinitarian form of their prayer testified to that conviction. An emergent ecumenical consensus understands eucharistic prayer to
unfold something like this:[2]

Opening Dialogue
The Preface:
> Thanksgiving to the Father for the marvels of creation, redemption, and
> sanctification (deriving from the Jewish tradition of the *berakah*).
>
> This Thanksgiving concludes with the singing of the Sanctus (Holy,
> Holy, Holy), from Isaiah 6, and the Benedictus, drawn from Psalm
> 118.

The Post-Sanctus (or Anamnesis):
> A memorial of the great acts of redemption, the passion, death, resurrec-
> tion, and ascension of Christ, and Pentecost, which brought the
> church into being.[3]
>
> The Words of Christ's Institution of the sacrament according to New
> Testament tradition.
>
> A Memorial Acclamation (e.g., Christ has died, Christ is risen, Christ will
> come again).

The Invocation of the Holy Spirit (Epiclesis) on the community and on the
elements of bread and wine.
> Consecration of the faithful to God.

Reference to the communion of saints.

Prayer for the return of the Lord and the definitive manifestation of his kingdom.

Trinitarian doxology.

The Amen of the whole community.

The Lord's Prayer.

Some churches vary this order slightly, by using the Words of Institution before the anamnesis rather than at its conclusion, or by using them as a warrant before the prayer, or as words of delivery after it; and others by invoking the Holy Spirit before the Words of Institution rather than following them, or in both places, once asking a blessing upon the community and once asking a blessing on the bread and cup. Some service books offer the option of including the intercessions (prayers of the church, prayers of the people) within the eucharistic prayer, at the conclusion of the epiclesis, before the Trinitarian doxology. Nevertheless, the structure of the prayer, variations not withstanding, is tripartite, or Trinitarian, as are the ecumenical creeds, focusing on Father, Son, and Holy Spirit. Even the variations testify to a remarkable ecumenical consensus as to the substantive contents of eucharistic prayer.

The contents of the eucharistic prayer as it has developed ecumenically lift up those biblical affirmations that lie at the heart of Christian faith. Though they may be understood differently in different eras, or by different confessional traditions, or by each of us as we grow in and into that faith, they are, nevertheless, the affirmations with which we always have to do.

Genuinely Christian faith cannot bypass incarnation, death and resurrection, ascension, session at God's right hand, or the Parousia. Whatever may be fashionable in academic or popular theology, classical forms of eucharistic prayer will not let us forget those affirmations upon which both Christian doctrine and Christian piety are based. This in itself is a strong argument for the ecumenical model.

1

Early Eucharistic Prayer

We "modern" human beings have difficulty recognizing that many of our basic assumptions about the world and how things work are not universal, or even inevitable. An anthropologist visiting our society from some centuries hence would be likely to identify the way our culture perceives the world as one possibility among many. A student of intellectual or social history might trace the connections that have shaped the "enlightened" Western worldview and note as well how that worldview becomes altered as society and culture change. The single most influential force in the shaping of the modern mind has been the intellectual movement that finally permeated the whole of Western society, the Enlightenment.

In our society, shaped as it has been by an Enlightenment perspective, very little room has been allowed for religious ritual. Ritual has been characterized as a primitive substitute for what might better be grasped by the intellect. A typical view is that Christianity began in utter simplicity, not burdened by rite, only to become complicated by later (and perhaps unfortunate) accretions. It is easy to presume that Jesus' Last Supper with his disciples was devoid of any but the barest of rituals, and that when Jesus instructed his disciples to "do this" in remembrance of him, he was simply creating a device which they might use to jog their memory of him after he was gone. This point of view is simply mistaken. As a practicing Jew, Jesus knew and participated in a liturgical tradition. He was not unfamiliar with ritual or disdainful of it, although, along with the Hebrew prophets, he was certainly critical of those who divorced worship from life in the world. At the Last Supper, as at every meal, Jesus prayed as a Jew.

JEWISH CEREMONIAL MEALS

Luke's account of the Last Supper reports Jesus as saying, "Then he took a loaf of bread, and when he had given thanks (*eucharistesas*), he broke it and gave it to them, saying, 'This is my body, which is given for you. Do this in remembrance (*anamnesin*) of me'" (Luke 22:19). Our word "Eucharist" comes from the Greek word *eucharistein*, to give thanks. Matthew and Mark report the institution of the Supper with a slight difference. They say, "While they were eating, Jesus took a loaf of bread, and after blessing (*eulogesas*) it he broke it, etc." (Matt. 26:26 and Mark 14:22). Whether he blessed (*eulogesas*) or gave thanks (*eucharistesas*), the point is that Jesus prayed over the food, and he prayed as Jews prayed at meals. This is the origin of the eucharistic prayer, or Great Thanksgiving. We cannot know precisely what Jesus said in his prayer, nor is it necessary for us to claim to know it, as though we were obligated to reproduce it. However, we do have some idea of Jewish table rituals and of the forms of prayers at meals. Jews did not approach these rituals and prayers casually or carelessly. Guests at a Jewish meal would be able to anticipate more or less what the host would say and do at the meal, even if the host did not follow an exact form of words.

When Jews sat down at the table together, they sat down as before God. They engaged in a holy thing. They did so not by improvising from scratch, but guided by a protocol rooted in tradition. Written liturgical texts related to Jewish meal rituals don't appear until after Jesus' time, so scholars can't be as confident of the first-century forms as they would like. It's quite likely, however, that more or less standardized practices preceded their reduction to written texts, so first-century forms might not have been terribly different from those later put in writing.

It's not certain whether the Last Supper was a Passover meal. The three Synoptic Gospels (Matthew, Mark, and Luke) identify it as such, while John does not. In any case, every Jewish meal was a religious event. The Passover meal essentially followed the same protocol as at other ceremonial meals, with the addition of certain symbolic foods and the ritual dialogue called the *haggadah*. The meal in the upper room, described in the Synoptic Gospels, could be any ceremonial meal. It would have begun with ritual handwashing. Then each arriving guest would have been given a cup of wine. Luke's narrative of the institution of the Lord's Supper, unlike the other three Gospels, specifically mentions this first cup, which immediately precedes the meal (Luke 22:17). The guest would drink it, repeating this blessing: "Blessed be thou, JHWH, our God, King of the universe, who givest us this fruit of the vine."[1]

The official beginning of the meal would have occurred when the host or the presiding member of the community broke the bread, offering this blessing: "Blessed be thou, JHWH, our God, King of the universe, who bringest forth bread from the earth."[2] After this general blessing that inaugurated the meal, latecomers were not allowed to take part. Various courses and cups of wine followed, with the several participants offering appropriate blessings over each. At the end of the meal, there was another handwashing. (Perhaps this was the place where, in John's Gospel, Jesus washed the disciples' feet.)

The chief prayer of the meal was a *birkat-ha-mazon*—a prayer recited in thanksgiving at the end of the meal over a final cup of wine—the "cup of blessing." The presider, with the cup of wine mixed with water before him,

> solemnly invited those assisting to join in with his act of thanksgiving. "Let us give thanks to the Lord our God," he said. . . . They then answered in a similar vein: "Blessed be he whose generosity has given us food and whose kindness has given us life.[3]

The host or other presider chanted a series of blessings (*berakoth*), the first of which blesses God for the food and nourishment provided by the meal and then expands into "a cosmic blessing for all of creation."[4] The second *berakah* blesses God for the gift of the land of promise and expands to include thanksgiving for the covenant and the Torah, in other words, for the whole history of salvation. The third *berakah* beseeches God to continue today the same creative and redemptive works as in the times of Israel's forebears and prays for the fulfillment of the divine purpose, indeed, that the Messiah may come and the kingdom of God be established. It concludes with a doxology of praise.[5]

The apostle Paul was quite probably describing the *birkat-ha-mazon* when he wrote "The cup of blessing that we bless, is it not a sharing in the blood of Christ?" (1 Cor. 10:16). We are on speculative ground when we try to re-create the precise nature of rites and prayers at the Last Supper or even in the earliest eucharistic praying of the church. Are the rites and prayers of Jewish tradition that were only later put into writing sufficient clues to patterns of Jewish prayer a century or two earlier? Was the earliest eucharistic prayer more influenced by Jewish patterns of blessing (*berakah*) or of thanksgiving (*todah*)?

Thomas Talley suggests that the *birkat-ha-mazon* probably served as the pattern of early eucharistic prayer: praise, thanksgiving, and supplication. The dominant note became thanksgiving rather than blessing (i.e., *todah* rather than *berakah*, *eucharistesas* rather than *eulogesas*) because of the Christian focus on Christ's glorious work of redemption.[6]

Some Jewish communities recited all the Hallel psalms (psalms of praise, Psalms 113 through 118) after the evening meal. This may have been the "hymn" that the Gospel writers tell us the disciples sang after they had eaten in the upper room.

THE PRAYERS OF THE SYNAGOGUE SERVICE

Of course, Christian eucharistic prayer may have drawn upon other models than the relatively familiar Jewish meal prayers.[7] Another possible model is the prayers of the synagogue service. At the heart of the daily service were the *Shemoneh Esreh*, the Eighteen Benedictions. They began with three *berakoth* (blessings), followed by twelve supplications, each one ending with a brief *berakah* (blessing), and the whole concluding with three more *berakoth*. Although passed down at first by oral tradition, they had "a content, a structure and key terms that were perfectly defined from the outset."[8] Typically, blessings begin with a formula that is nearly always the same: "Blessed (art) thou, Adonai, our God, king of the ages (or 'of the universe')."[9]

The first of the Eighteen Benedictions thanks God for the forebears with whom the covenant was made, and anticipates the coming of the Messiah. The second gives thanks for life and for the hope of the resurrection. The third blesses the divine name. Jewish prayer, whether in the synagogue service or at meals, tends to be rooted in praise and thanksgiving to God for creation and for acts of redemption, specifically recalled, and in supplications for continued blessings, particularly for the coming of the Messiah. Whatever the exact content of Jesus' prayer at the Last Supper, it was certainly shaped by Jewish precedent. Most likely his prayer included at least the bipartite form of thanksgiving and supplication, or it may have taken the tripartite form of praise, thanksgiving, and petition.[10]

THE ROLE OF REMEMBERED HISTORY IN BIBLICAL RELIGION

Biblical religion is different from nature religions in that it is historically oriented. Rather than focusing on universals such as birth and death, the forces of nature, and times of dormancy and renewal, biblical faith centers on God's actions in history. Both Jews and Christians have discerned God's hand at work in the call to Abraham and Sarah; Moses and the exodus; the Babylonian exile; the time-specific ministries of the prophets; the birth, ministry, death, and resurrection of Jesus Christ; the work of the apostles; and the anticipation of a consummation of history yet to come. While the Bible contains hymns, poetry, parables, proverbs, and other kinds of literature, historical reflection carries the narrative forward. Of course, the Bible does not record "history" in the same way that contemporary historians claim to do it. The biblical narratives make no attempt at being neutral or detached. They do not simply report events but interpret them. They "see" God at work in affairs that could be described quite differently if there were no reference to God. Both the biblical writers and believing readers see with the eyes of faith, but their sight is fixed not on mythological events, but on events that occur in historical time, and on events they believe God has promised in future time.

For example, the Deuteronomist records a confession of faith that the Hebrew people may have recited at harvest time. It begins, "A wandering Aramean was my ancestor . . . ," then rehearses the history of bondage in Egypt, the exodus, and the giving of the land (Deut. 26:5).

Similarly, Psalms 105 and 106 recite the mighty acts of God: "Then Israel came to Egypt. . . . Then he brought Israel out. . . . He spread a cloud for a covering, and fire to give light by night. . . . He gave them food from heaven. . . . He gave them the lands of the nations" (Ps. 105: 23, 37, 39, 40, 44).

The need for some sort of proclamation of God's saving acts in history is deeply rooted in biblical tradition and continues in the New Testament. One example is Stephen's sermon before the council (Acts 7:1–53): "The God of glory appeared to our ancestor Abraham. . . . The patriarchs, jealous of Joseph, sold him into Egypt. . . . Moses was born" (Acts 7:2, 9, 20). Stephen speaks of Joshua, David, Solomon, and the prophets, leading to an accusing reference to the encounter of the religious authorities with Jesus: "And now you have become his betrayers and murderers" (Acts 7:52).

From Old Testament to New, biblical narrative played a significant role in Jewish ways of praying. The apostle Paul, as a Jew himself, certainly was steeped in Jewish habits of prayer, and his writings give evidence of having been influenced by the tradition. He typically begins a letter with some sort of thanksgiving accompanied by testimony to some action that exhibits God's faithfulness, often moving on to petition. In the letter to the Philippians, Paul writes,

> I thank my God every time I remember you. . . . I am confident of this, that the one who began a good work among you will bring it to completion. . . . And this is my prayer, that your love may overflow more and more.[11]

This pattern of blessing/thanking, recollection of God's redemptive action among God's people, and petition that God may continue to be faithful to the people of God links some Jewish patterns of prayer with eucharistic prayer as it developed in the church.

POST–NEW TESTAMENT ACCOUNTS
OF THE LORD'S SUPPER

The earliest references to the Lord's Supper outside the New Testament are few and sketchy. In the *Didache*, which most scholars date in the first quarter of the second century, Chapter Nine seems to be a Christianization of the blessing over the first cup, which preceded the Jewish meal (you will recall that in the Synoptic Gospels, only Luke makes mention of this cup [Luke 22:17]): "We give thee thanks, our Father, for the holy vine of David thy servant, which thou hast made known to us through Jesus thy servant; to thee be glory forever."[12] Immediately following is a prayer over the bread, which in a Jewish setting would serve as the general thanksgiving that marks the beginning of the meal.

The prayer that most resembles later eucharistic prayers appears in Chapter Ten of the *Didache*, preceded by the instruction, "And when you are filled give thanks thus."[13] It seems to be modeled on the *birkat-ha-mazon*, the prayer after the meal over the "cup of blessing," but adapted for Christian use. It begins with thanksgiving for the knowledge of God revealed in Christ, with an ascription of praise. Then it specifically thanks God for the creation, especially food and drink, and most especially for the spiritual food and drink that leads to eternal life. There follows a petition that God remember the church, protect it from evil, perfect it in the divine love, and gather it into the kingdom. The prayer concludes with a doxology, and "Hosanna to the son of David." An invitation is offered, with a caution: "If one is holy, let him come; if not, let him repent." The last word is "Maranatha"—Lord, come! After the prayer comes a rubric: "But permit the prophets to give thanks as much as they will."[14] Most likely, there was a familiar structure to the prayer, but no precise text, so that "the prophets" might expand the praise, thanksgiving, and petition within the structure.

Justin Martyr, writing from Rome about the middle of the second century, provided brief descriptions of Christian worship for those unfamiliar with it. In the *First Apology*, Justin writes of the Lord's Day assembly that bread is presented, and wine with water; the president likewise offers up prayers and thanksgivings according to his ability.[15] More specifically, the "president of the brethren"

> sends up praise and glory to the Father of all, through the name of the Son and Holy Spirit, and offers thanksgiving at some length. . . . When he has finished the prayers and the thanksgiving, all the people present shout their assent, saying, "Amen."[16]

In the *Dialogue with Trypho*, Justin observed further:

> We give thanks to God for having created the world, with all things therein, for the sake of man; and for delivering us from the evil in which we live; and for utterly overthrowing the principalities and powers, through Him who suffered according to His will.[17]

CHRISTIAN REWORKING OF JEWISH PATTERNS OF PRAYER

From all appearances, it would seem that the early Christians created their own prayers of thanksgiving by adding the name of Jesus in juxtaposition to the traditional themes of Jewish prayer. Since Jewish prayer typically included a recital of the mighty acts of God, it was reasonable that Christians would see the coming of Christ as the culmination of God's redemptive action in history.[18] Christian thanksgiving at the eucharistic meal may or may not have aspired to follow the model of Jesus' table prayers, but the evangelists in their reports of the Last Supper described only that part of the rite that was new and related specifically to Jesus. The Gospel writers do not report details of the prayer, which in all likelihood would have been basically familiar to Jewish readers in its basic outline, but mention only those new things that Jesus had added to the traditional table prayers on the occasion of the Last Supper.[19]

Whereas in Jewish prayer one of the "blessings" was in the form of thanksgiving for creation, covenant, and the land, in Christian prayer all these come together in God's gift of Jesus Christ. If he is the true bread from heaven and the true vine, then thanks must be given for him rather than, as formerly, for the land and for the line of David.[20]

Whether direct or indirect, there seems to be a clear relationship between Jewish prayer, both in the synagogue and at meals, and Christian eucharistic prayer. Each begins with blessing or thanking God for creation and life itself, as well as for God's faithfulness to God's people in times past, as recalled in the rehearsal of historical narrative. Each moves toward petition, asking God to remember and be faithful to the divine promise, especially the promise of eschatological consummation in the kingdom of God. In particular, the Jewish meal prayers, focusing especially on the cup and the loaf, lead to the Christian eucharistic prayers, in which special significance is attached to cup and loaf as representing Jesus himself, as well as the messianic banquet to be enjoyed with him in the kingdom.

Probably the oldest text of a eucharistic prayer is one attributed to Hippolytus of Rome in *Apostolic Tradition*, about AD 215.[21] It begins with thanksgiving specifically for "your beloved Servant, Jesus Christ," and recalls his conception, incarnation, suffering, and resurrection, leading to a recital of the Words of Institution. A prayer for the Holy Spirit follows, that the Spirit may descend upon the church's offering, gather all the faithful in unity, fill them, and confirm their faith in the truth. The prayer concludes with a Trinitarian doxology. This is the first known example of a prayer that includes the Words of Institution. Ancient eucharistic prayers usually mention what the Lord instituted, without quoting the precise words.[22] The accent in Hippolytus's prayer is on the work of the Holy Spirit, whose action delivered to the communicants the fruits of Holy Communion, although there was no suggestion of a "consecration" as such.[23]

DEVELOPING PATTERNS OF EUCHARISTIC PRAYER

The use of an explicit prayer for the Holy Spirit would become a distinctive mark of the eucharistic prayers of the Eastern church. It corresponds to a trend of Orthodox theology, beginning at an early stage, to consider the Holy Spirit as "the executor and accomplisher of every divine work."[24] At this point the theology of Calvin finds an especially strong link to Orthodoxy, as we shall see.

The eucharistic prayer developed somewhat differently in the various Christian centers. Those who presided at the Eucharist customarily prayed using their own words but following established precedents, which developed as six major traditions, identifiable as West Syrian (Antioch, Jerusalem), East Syrian (Syria, Iraq), Egyptian (Alexandria), Byzantine (derived from Antioch), Armenian, and Roman. By the fourth century, perhaps as early as AD 300, the Antiochene tradition formed the prayer in a tripartite, or Trinitarian, form, "where an opening praise of God as Creator leads into Sanctus, and is followed by a christological thanksgiving and a pneumatological supplication."[25]

The oldest text of a eucharistic prayer that has continued in use is from the East Syrian tradition, the Anaphora of Addai and Mari. (Eastern Christians have used the word "anaphora" [offering] in reference to the eucharistic prayer, whereas in the West it came to be called the "canon.") The Anaphora of Addai and Mari, which dates from as early as the third century, includes thanksgiving for creation, an abbreviated Sanctus, an Anamnesis (recollection of God's redemptive work in Christ), and an Epiclesis (prayer for the Holy Spirit), but no Words of Institution.

Although one person (the bishop, who was in the beginning the local pastor) presided at prayer, just as one person presided over the prayers of the Jewish meal, the whole assembly added their voices in song, as most likely was also the case at a Jewish table. In Christian eucharistic praying, tradition favored specific sung acclamations drawn from Scripture and, in some cases, from Jewish liturgical practice, such as the Sanctus, the Benedictus, and the final Amen in response to the closing doxology.

We don't know the precise history of the use of the Sanctus,[26] although it is obviously drawn from Scripture (Isa. 6:3) and may have been used as part of the synagogue liturgy, perhaps included in the *berakah* that immediately preceded the *Shema*.[27] Possibly it was introduced into Christian liturgy as a means of linking one movement of the eucharistic prayer to another. A piece of writing dating from the end of the fourth or beginning of the fifth century declared that the Sanctus was used in all of the Eastern churches and some of the churches of the West. Its use in Christian liturgy probably originated in Jerusalem and Antioch, although some favor an Egyptian origin. Since at least the seventh century, the Roman Canon has customarily added to the Sanctus the Benedictus, from Psalm 118:26.[28]

THE ANTIOCHENE/CONTEMPORARY MODEL

The Antiochene prayers most often serve as the model for contemporary eucharistic prayers. Eucharistic prayers originating in Antioch are conspicuously Trinitarian, making use of a tripartite form.[29] Eucharistic prayers in other areas, such as Rome, were likely to follow a bipartite form, combining thanksgiving and supplication throughout.[30] Typically, a West Syrian (Antiochene) prayer begins with the Preface. In this case, the Preface is not something that precedes something else, but rather a kind of proclamation. In the Preface, the church praises and thanks God for the work of creation and for God's mighty acts, including the coming of Christ, and reaches a high point in the Sanctus, meant to be sung by the whole congregation. The second movement of the prayer, called the Post-Sanctus or the Anamnesis, recalls salvation history specifically as it has taken shape in Jesus Christ and leads to the institution narrative. In the third part of the prayer, called the Epiclesis (calling upon), the church beseeches God to send the Holy Spirit upon the gifts of bread and wine and upon the people gathered. It was typical in the Eastern churches to include at this point the intercessions. The prayer concludes with a Trinitarian doxology. The Antiochene form of prayer has commended itself because it flows clearly as a single prayer from beginning to end, evokes Jewish and early Christian modes of prayer, and is clearly Trinitarian and doxological.

Basil of Caesarea (AD 329–79) brought the core of his eucharistic prayer from Alexandria. His prayer includes the earliest known appearance of the Lord's Prayer in a eucharistic text.[31] The Lord's Prayer may have been considered a summing-up of the anaphora, as it follows a similar form, also bearing the marks of Jewish prayer. The Lord's Prayer begins, of course, by blessing God ("hallowed be thy name"), followed by petitions, including one for the eschatological consummation ("thy kingdom come").

Eucharistic prayers tended to become fixed in the post-Nicene era. By the fourth century, prayers began to be written down. In written form, the prayers in use in one center became available to churches in other centers, and mutual influences become evident, leading to more uniformity of structure and contents and, sometimes, even phraseology. Travel between the major centers also became more frequent beginning in the fourth century, leading to familiarity with one another's manner of praying the Eucharist. While earlier practice had been shaped by local tradition and by the particular gifts of the presider, the great theological debates of the fourth century required greater precision in the texts. Quite probably, the great influx of new church members after Constantine also contributed to the fixing of permanent eucharistic forms of prayer. Small assemblies turned into large ones, often in large meeting places, and the need for consistency and reliability may have encouraged the use of authoritative forms.

Should we consider the evolution of eucharistic prayer into fixed rather than fluid forms to be an unfortunate imposition of centralizing authority, even a symptom of decline? Or might we consider it a sign of developing theological and liturgical maturity? Given the crises of the fourth century, requiring the church to clarify its faith with respect to one challenge after another, often striking at the very heart of the gospel; and given the sudden enlargement of the church with the addition of multitudes after the church became favored by Constantine's empire, it would seem as though a careful and thoughtful attention to the central prayer of the worshipping community was both necessary and essential to the integrity of the church's faith.

Nevertheless, while eucharistic prayer in the major Christian centers had always shared some content and frequently structural similarities, even the changes of the fourth century did not bring about uniformity. The sphere of Alexandria-Egypt projected the influence of the *Euchologion* of Bishop Sarapion of Thmuis, while the liturgy in the eighth book of the *Apostolic Constitutions* (also called the Clementine liturgy) underlay the tripartite form of Antioch-Syria. The Antiochene structure gained considerable influence when in AD 398 John Chrysostom introduced the liturgy that bears his name to the church of the eastern empire centered in Byzantium. Meanwhile, the prayer of the Roman church maintained its own distinctiveness. Like many earlier eucharistic prayers, the Roman Canon is a series of short prayers linked together. Eucharistic prayer, East and West, while having a good deal in common, also exhibits considerable diversity.

2

Eucharistic Prayer
in the Roman Tradition

Occasionally members or ministers in Reformed churches complain that our churches are becoming "too Catholic." Ironically, parishioners in Roman Catholic parishes sometimes lament that their church has become "too Protestant." Actually, both Protestants and Roman Catholics have approached convergence on many issues related to worship. The reason is not that one or both have set out to imitate the other, but that, from the late nineteenth century until the present day, scholars of both traditions have reexamined Scripture, historical developments, and ecumenical problems with special attention to what they disclose about the origins, theology, and practices of Christian worship. In the matter of eucharistic prayer, it is certain that twentieth- and twenty-first-century Reformed are not imitating traditional Roman Catholic patterns. Since Vatican Council II, Roman Catholic eucharistic prayer has faced changes at least as great as changes introduced in Reformed liturgies. Each tradition has moved away from earlier practice and toward models of eucharistic prayer that took shape before the great East-West division in the church, long before the Reformation of the sixteenth century.

We have only some of the many early eucharistic prayers. Justin Martyr's brief description of such prayer from the second century makes it clear that the presider "offers thanksgiving at some length," and that he did so "according to his ability." In other words, he framed the prayer in his own words. Although we presume that the presider followed a traditional pattern, and that the pattern was at least similar to patterns of eucharistic prayer in other places, no one can say for certain exactly what those early patterns looked like, even though the great likelihood is that they resembled Jewish practice at least in

11

some respects. However, we may say with more confidence that insofar as the patterns of early eucharistic prayers can be discerned in those prayers available to us, they bear some resemblance to the magnificent biblical recitations of the mighty acts of God (see chapter 1). They narrate the story of God's redemptive work, beginning with the creation and continuing through the death, resurrection, and ascension of Christ. For example, Hippolytus's eucharistic prayer dates from about AD 215. The earliest surviving text of a eucharistic prayer,[1] it gives thanks for Jesus Christ, the Word "through whom you made all things," then leads into an extensive recital of God's mighty acts in Jesus Christ.[2] This narrative style of eucharistic prayer leaves its mark on later prayers as their form becomes more fixed. This is particularly true in the evolution of the Antiochene form of eucharistic prayer, which in its clarity of form and content has provided the chief model for contemporary prayer at Eucharist.

ORIGINS OF THE ROMAN CANON

The eucharistic prayer of the traditional Roman rite is called the "Canon." The contemporary, post–Vatican II Sacramentary has added three other general eucharistic prayers as options, three eucharistic prayers for use with children, and two on the theme of reconciliation. None of these new prayers follows the model of the Roman Canon, but they more nearly resemble the Antiochene forms as, for example, do the Great Thanksgivings in the 1993 Presbyterian *Book of Common Worship*. However, the Sacramentary identifies the Roman Canon as "Eucharistic Prayer 1," obviously holding the place of honor.[3] (See Appendix C.)

The Roman Canon prayed today as Eucharistic Prayer 1 is substantially the same eucharistic prayer that was in use at the time of the Reformation, although there was considerably more variety in the pre-Reformation church than one might imagine. While the rites of the city of Rome enjoyed special status, other dioceses followed regional patterns. Before the Reformation, depending on local custom, the Mass might be prayed using Celtic, Mozarabic, Milanese, or other forms, sometimes lumped together as a species under the label "Gallican." Diversity is evident particularly in the Prefaces, but also in those portions of the prayer designated as "Communicantes" and "Hanc igitur." Only in the Counter-Reformation did the Council of Trent (1545–63) set limits to diversity. The image of Roman Catholic liturgy as monolithic stems from the Tridentine efforts to establish a single, authoritative rite.

While most Reformed and other Protestant churches have chosen, in their recent liturgical materials, to follow the Antiochene model, and the newer

Roman Catholic eucharistic prayers follow a modified version of it, the old Roman Canon does not.[4] The eucharistic prayer as it would have been prayed in Roman Catholic churches at the time of the Reformation has an entirely different form, in which narrative plays a decidedly subordinate role when compared to Eastern prayers. Proper Prefaces, of which there were many, may sometimes have included brief historical narrative, as does also the Qui pridie, that prayer of the Canon that includes the institution narrative, reciting the story of the Last Supper.[5] Likewise, the Unde et Memores recalls Christ's passion, resurrection, and ascension. However, the creation, the exodus, and the work of the prophets typically have no place in the Roman Canon, and even the christological narratives are brief. None of the narrative attempts a full summary of salvation history. In contrast to prayers of the Eastern type, the reduced use of narrative in the Roman Canon may help to explain why doxology is not the dominant tone.

The origins of the Roman Canon are obscure, although scholars have traced a connection with the ancient Liturgy of St. Mark, associated with the see of Alexandria, in Egypt. The first full text of a Roman Canon appeared in the Gelasian Sacramentary (AD 750), although the core of it may have existed by the end of the fourth century. By the thirteenth century, the Canon had reached the relatively fixed form it manifests today. It more nearly resembles a series of prayers, each complete in itself, than a single, unified prayer. It begins with the familiar opening dialogue.

> The Lord be with you.
> **And also with you.**
>
> Lift up your hearts.
> **We lift them to the Lord.**
>
> Let us give thanks to the Lord our God.
> **It is right to give him thanks and praise.**

The Preface (Latin "praefatio") comes immediately after the dialogue, beginning with "It is truly right, just, proper and helpful toward salvation, that we always and everywhere give thanks to you, O Lord, holy Father, almighty and eternal God, through Christ our Lord."[6] The Preface continues, offering thanks to God and reciting the reasons for such thanksgiving. "Preface" does not have the literal meaning we usually associate with that word, that is, something preceding something else. It comes closer to meaning "proclamation." In early centuries the word "Preface" often referred to the whole eucharistic prayer. In time, however, it came to stand for that part of the prayer immediately after the opening dialogue, and concluding with the Sanctus ("Holy, holy, holy Lord . . .").

THE PRAYERS OF THE ROMAN CANON

The Prefaces of the Roman Canon vary with time and occasion (thus the term "Proper Prefaces," indicating a linkage specifically to themes of the liturgical year, e.g., Advent, Christmas, Lent, Easter, or to special services related to marriage, funerals, etc.). Until 1968, the official missal had only fourteen prefaces. In a Sunday missal published before Vatican II to aid the laity in following the Latin Mass, neither the single Sunday Preface nor the one weekday Preface recalls events in salvation history. However, the contemporary Roman Sacramentary provides eighty-nine Proper Prefaces, each beginning with an address to God, saying, "We do well always and everywhere to give you thanks," then moving to some specific reference related to the day, season, or occasion, sometimes drawn from salvation history, sometimes not.

After the Sanctus comes the First Prayer of the Canon (known as "Te igitur," for the first words of the Latin prayer). From about the eighth century, the presider began at this point to utter the Canon in a low voice, basically inaudibly.[7] As the people were excluded from the hearing of the prayer, even church architecture was affected, as the altar was moved to the rear wall, as distant from the people as possible. Under the influence of multiple private masses, it had become the custom for the priest to take all the parts previously reserved for the people. At a high mass, the choir chanted psalms and orations throughout the Canon, but without any direct relation to it. Their chant simply covered the prayers of the priest.[8] A variety of sources offered allegorical interpretations of every gesture made by the priest, based on little more than imagination, and focused primarily on the suffering of the Lord.[9] The allegories differed from commentator to commentator, often contradicting each other.

The Te igitur asks God to accept the gifts, offerings, and sacrifices being offered for the church, and offered specifically for the pope, the local bishop, "and for all who hold and teach the catholic faith that comes to us from the apostles."[10]

The Second Prayer of the Canon ("Memento, Domine") is one of intercession. When a stipend was given for the mass, the one who gave it would be particularly remembered, while the prayer also makes a general reference to the congregation present, asking special blessings upon them and their loved ones.

The Third Prayer of the Canon ("Communicantes") is a continuation of the Memento, declaring the unity of the whole church in *koinonia* with all the saints, naming first "Mary, Mother of Our God and Lord, Jesus Christ," then reciting two lists of names, twelve apostles and twelve martyrs. It ends, "Through Christ our Lord. Amen," indicating that it brings the first section of intercessory prayer to a close. At the end of this prayer, a bell was rung as a signal that the act of consecration was approaching.[11]

The Fourth Prayer ("Hanc igitur") originated as an independent prayer, added to the Canon only later. This is a variable prayer, in which mention might be made of the special intention of the particular celebration. Like the Memento, it may identify by name specific persons who have sponsored the mass with an intention in mind. (Since these special intentions were sometimes trivial and even embarrassing, church authorities eventually ruled that they not be mentioned aloud.) The prayer asks God to accept "this offering of our worship and that of your whole household" and prays for peace in this life and salvation from "eternal damnation," again ending, "Through Christ our Lord. Amen." The contemporary version of this prayer is variable, depending on the day and liturgical season.

The Fifth Prayer of the Canon ("Quam oblationem") prays that "this offering" may "become for us the body and blood of your most beloved Son, our Lord Jesus Christ. Through Christ our Lord. Amen." Since it comes immediately before the institution narrative, it may have originated as a kind of heightened rhetoric serving as a transition leading to the sacred words. This prayer comes closer to a traditional Epiclesis than any other in the Canon. However, it is a prayer not merely for Christ's presence in the sacrament, but also for Christ's presence as the church's sacrificial offering.[12] The tradition of calling upon divine power *before* the institution narrative is the tradition of Alexandria (Egypt) and Rome, whereas the Antiochene tradition located its Epiclesis *after* the *verba*. This may seem a small matter, but it was a significant difference between the Eastern and Western churches.

Quam oblationem, tu Deus, in omnibus quaesumus, benedictam adscriptam ratam rationabilem, acceptabilemque facere digneris: ut nobis Corpus et Sanguis fiat dilectissimi Filii tui Domini nostri Jesu Christi.	We pray you, O God, be pleased to make this offering wholly blessed, to consecrate and approve it, making it reasonable and acceptable, so that it may become for us the body and blood of your most beloved Son, our Lord Jesus Christ.[13]

THE *VERBA*—WORDS OF INSTITUTION

The Sixth Prayer ("Qui pridie") includes the Words of Institution for the bread as an act of consecration, with particular attention given to "Hoc est enim corpus meum," "For this is my body." It does not include the words "which is given for you," although those words had appeared in earlier versions of the Canon. Jungmann estimates that they must have been removed sometime between the fourth and the seventh centuries.

Then, beginning with "Simili modo" ("in the same manner"), come the Words of Institution for the cup. In the Latin Mass, the words "For this is the cup of my blood of the new and everlasting covenant" were followed immediately by the words "Mysterium fidei" ("The mystery of faith"). No one knows the origin or significance of placing this affirmation here. The contemporary form of the Roman Canon, as adopted by Vatican Council II, separates "Mysterium fidei" from its original position immediately following the *verba* for the cup and frames it as an invitation: "Let us proclaim the mystery of faith." This is the model for what the contemporary liturgies of many denominations designate as the Memorial Acclamation.[14] It is one of the few places where contemporary rites borrow from the Roman Canon. However, the Eastern anaphoras traditionally include acclamations after the Words of Institution, and these have served as a model for the contemporary, post–Vatican II version of the Canon, as well as for Protestant versions of the Memorial Acclamation.[15] The most striking similarity is found in The (Syriac) Anaphora of the Twelve Apostles, in which, immediately after the *verba*, the presider prays, "Your death, O Lord, we commemorate and your resurrection we confess and your second coming we await."[16]

Although not taken directly from any of the scriptural accounts, the Words of Institution as cited in the Canon come closest to the words used in Matthew's account of the Last Supper (Matt. 26:26–29), because Matthew includes the phrase "for the forgiveness of sins," which does not appear in the versions recorded in Mark, Luke, or 1 Corinthians 11. The Canon, however, makes no eschatological reference, as do all three Synoptics and the Pauline epistle when citing the Words of Institution.[17] The fact that the Words of Institution are not direct quotes from any one text reflects early tradition, in which eucharistic prayers were more likely to allude to Scripture or paraphrase it than quote from it directly.

"Unde et memores" is, in the strictest meaning of the term, an Anamnesis, a memorial of Christ's sacrifice before God, but it is also an oblation of Christ to the Father, commending the offering of the gifts God has bestowed on us, and particularly recalling Christ's passion, his resurrection, and his ascension.

"Supra quae" asks that God look with favor upon the gifts being offered, accepting them as God accepted the offerings of Abel, Abraham, and the high priest Melchizedek. Then follows the prayer, "Supplices": "Almighty God, bid these offerings be carried by the hands of your holy angel to your altar on high," ending once again, "Through the same Christ our Lord. Amen." Supplices is sometimes taken as another form of the Epiclesis, although, when it prays that an angel might carry the offerings "up" to the heavenly altar, the direction of the action is reversed from the traditional Epiclesis, which calls upon the Spirit to "come down," so to speak, and bless "us and these gifts of bread and wine." The Supplices also prays for a fruitful communion by the congregation, that they might receive Christ's body and blood, and "be filled with every grace and heavenly blessing."

Prayer is offered for the dead ("Memento etiam, Domine"), who can no longer participate in the Eucharist but who "have gone before us with the sign of faith," "sign" referring to their baptism. In their deaths, they have completed their baptisms. The Memento offers the opportunity of naming specific persons. The prayer beginning "Ipsis, Domine" continues the theme of remembrance of the dead, asking God for rest and refreshment for those who have died in Christ. Once again, the prayer ends, "Through Christ our Lord. Amen."

The "Nobis quoque" beseeches God that "your sinful servants" might also share in the fellowship of the apostles and martyrs. "Sinful servants" is a self-identification of the priest and his assistants. The prayer names particular apostles and martyrs, beginning with "John" [the Baptist], then listing seven men, followed by seven women. The prayer concludes by begging God that we, forgiven sinners, might share in their heavenly company, with the prayer ending "Through Christ our Lord."

The prayer beginning "Per quem haec omnia" is an act of praise, offered "Through Christ our Lord. Through him you give us all these gifts." The accent is on God's gifts descending to us from heaven.

The Canon closes with the great Trinitarian doxology, in which the movement is reversed from that of the preceding prayer, this time with honor and glory ascending from us to God, rather than descending: "Through him, with him, in him, in the unity of the Holy Spirit, all glory and honor is yours, almighty Father, for ever and ever. Amen." This closing doxology resembles the one with which the eucharistic prayer attributed to Hippolytus closes.[18] The Lord's Prayer, with its petitions, "thy kingdom come," and "give us this day our daily bread," follows.

COMPARISONS WITH EASTERN FORMS

It is evident that the Roman Canon differs considerably from the eucharistic prayers of the Eastern anaphoras, which, however they may have been constructed from independent prayers, gradually adopted transitions designed to create a unitary impression. The Canon does not have a Trinitarian form. There is no Epiclesis as such, specifically praying for the presence and action of the Holy Spirit, although the Quam oblationem is similar in function. The

Canon has no eschatological horizon. Although it prays that the faithful may escape damnation, and prays for the dead, and for "some share in the fellowship of your apostles and martyrs," it includes no references to the kingdom of God, to the new heaven and earth, or to the consummation of all things. There is considerable repetition of themes, and an overall impression that a variety of prayers from diverse sources have become linked together without being truly melded into one. The chief emphasis is on petition, with a variety of intercessions dispersed throughout, and with doxological themes muted. Perhaps more important, the Canon lacks a narrative structure that rehearses the history of salvation, leaving what little there is mostly to the Preface.

One Catholic scholar's critique is that the themes of offering and God's acceptance of the offering are exaggerated in the Roman Canon.[19] Certainly, the focus on sacrifice drew the critical attention of the Protestant reformers. Nevertheless, the Canon exhibits a disciplined, simple, and elegant use of language. Because it offers "Proper" variations in the Preface and elsewhere, it is more flexible than the fixed anaphoras common in the East, offering the possibility of directly relating the prayer to seasons and occasions.

Whatever the merits or faults of the Roman Canon, it has not served as a model either for the optional eucharistic prayers provided in the twentieth-century Roman Sacramentary or for those in contemporary Protestant service books. It is not structurally similar to the Eastern anaphoras. Why did the fathers of the Second Vatican Council depart from the form of the Roman Canon in the preparation of new eucharistic prayers? Archbishop Annibale Bugnini (1912–82) served in leadership capacities on commissions related to the liturgy and liturgical reform from 1948 to 1969, and then from 1969 to 1975 as Secretary of the Vatican's Congregation for Divine Worship. In his record of decisions related to the eucharistic prayer, he reports that the Council chose to authorize eucharistic prayers in addition to the Roman Canon because historical study made it clear that in early centuries there was no one single prayer used at Eucharist, and even the Roman Canon originally had a number of variable texts.[20] These historical precedents lent legitimacy to the council fathers' feeling that variety would serve a positive good. Literary criticism of the Roman Canon also played a role.

> I mean that when the Roman Canon and other very old prayers "canonized" by centuries of liturgical tradition were subjected to a careful conceptual and stylistic analysis in light of the general principles of Vatican II and the comparative history of anaphoras, they revealed "numerous and serious . . . defects and limitations of structure."[21]

Perhaps more important was their desire to create eucharistic prayers that functioned more as a single prayer than as a series of prayers strung together.

The Commission on the Liturgy set out to determine what were the essential elements of a eucharistic prayer. They agreed on a common structure that should serve as the form of any new eucharistic prayers.

Preface

Transition from the *Sanctus* to the consecratory epiclesis

Consecratory epiclesis

Account of institution

Anamnesis and offering of the divine Victim

Prayer for acceptance of the offering and for a fruitful communion,

Commemoration of the saints and intercessions, and

Doxology[22]

This pattern is notably similar to the Antiochene form, with the exception of the placement of the Epiclesis. The commission deliberately placed the Epiclesis *before* the Words of Institution, imitating the order of the Roman Canon in which the Quam oblationem, which functions as a kind of Epiclesis, precedes the Qui pridie, the account of the institution. Consistent with Roman tradition, the weight of consecration falls on the Words of Institution instead of on the Epiclesis, so that the *verba* are not simply a prelude to "consecration." Nevertheless, it is worthy of note that the new prayers would include a very specific invocation of the Holy Spirit, following Eastern practice. At several points, the practice of the Eastern Orthodox churches served as a model, for example, for the congregational acclamation after the Words of Institution and for the placement of the intercessions and the commemorations of the saints.

The Commission on the Liturgy recommended the addition of still another eucharistic prayer, this one borrowed whole from the Eastern churches (including the Roman Catholic Uniate churches): the Alexandrian anaphora of St. Basil. The structure of that eucharistic prayer is easily recognizable as the typical Antiochene form:

thanksgiving for creation (down to the *Sanctus*);

thanksgiving for the whole history of salvation;

words of consecration *(institution narrative)*;

full anamnesis of the work of redemption . . . ;

epiclesis in its oldest form, in which the Holy Spirit is invoked in order that the gifts may be consecrated and the offerers may be sanctified and led, as a single body with a single spirit, to the full enjoyment of God's kingdom and the glorification of the entire Trinity;

short but universal intercessory prayer that all may be one in the building up of Christ's body and God's people;

great recapitulatory doxology.[23]

Some critics raised objections to the use of this eucharistic prayer, particularly on the grounds that the Epiclesis *follows* "the consecration" (i.e., the Words of Institution) instead of preceding it, which had to be a delicate matter, given the centuries of conflict between East and West over which form of words was essential for "consecration" to take place. Ultimately, higher authorities prevailed, and the anaphora from the Liturgy of St. Basil was rejected as an optional form of eucharistic prayer.

The three major eucharistic prayers ultimately added to the Roman Sacramentary include Eucharistic Prayer II, modeled on the prayer of Hippolytus of Rome, of which a version is also included in the 1993 *Book of Common Worship* as Great Thanksgiving G. This prayer is short and very simple. Eucharistic Prayer III, of medium length, takes care to include in the Anamnesis explicit reference to our expectation of the Lord's glorious return. Eucharistic Prayer IV is longer, providing a fuller recital of salvation history and clearly biblical in its images and use of language. Bugnini remarks that of the three new prayers, the fourth most closely approaches the Antiochene type. The chief difference is, as in the others, the placement of the Epiclesis. The work of Vatican Council II, then, while honoring the Roman Canon and continuing to give it first place in the Sacramentary, nevertheless turned in an ecumenical direction, borrowing from Eastern models of a unitary prayer with a fixed structure, while providing for the possibility of some variety.

At the time of the Reformation, both Reformed and Lutherans had turned away from the Canon to develop forms of eucharistic prayer more or less distant from it. Nevertheless, at least one aspect of the Canon left its mark on eucharistic praying in Protestant churches from the sixteenth century forward, and that is the role played by the Words of Institution. The Words of Institution have played such a significant role in both Catholic and Protestant eucharistic celebrations that many simply assume that they were a part of eucharistic praying from the beginning. However, as noted above, there are early eucharistic prayers that do not include the Words of Institution. In fact, according to Robert Taft, "there is not a single extant pre-Nicene eucharistic prayer that one can prove contained the Words of Institution."[24] In the Eastern church, the Words of Institution, while they came to be included, did not play nearly the central role that they played in the Roman Canon. From the Eastern point of view, the Epiclesis was far more critical to the prayer than the *verba*. If there were a moment of "consecration," it was at the Epiclesis, according to Cyril of Jerusalem. One cause of the persistent division between churches of East and West was that the church of Rome had come to see the Words of Institution as *the* essential of the eucharistic prayer, while the Orthodox could not conceive of a Eucharist without explicit prayer for the Holy Spirit. The Orthodox anaphoras placed the Epiclesis *after* the Words of Institution in order to make the theological point that the *verba* were not sufficient, by themselves, to "turn the Supper into a true eschatological event."[25]

Since early prayers did not always include the *verba*, it is curious that the Roman Catholic tradition came to see the Words of Institution as essential, identifying the precise moment when "consecration" (i.e., the act of transubstantiation) occurred. Apparently, this was not always so. No evidence exists that before the Middle Ages anyone identified a particular moment at which consecration took place. The common belief had been that the eucharistic prayer as a whole effected consecration.[26]

A series of papal decrees issued in the fourteenth and fifteenth centuries took a new turn, declaring the Words of Institution to be the essential moment of consecration.[27] Although this point of view seems to have originated with medieval scholastic theology and is often associated with Thomas Aquinas, rather than originating in the undivided church, it became the conventional teaching and would have been familiar to both Luther and Calvin.[28] However, contemporary Catholic teaching is more likely to take the older view, that is, that the entire eucharistic prayer effects consecration rather than the Words of Institution in isolation from it.[29]

The manner of celebrating the Eucharist among both Lutheran and Reformed from the sixteenth century forward has been shaped, it would seem, at least in part by the medieval and specifically Roman focus on the Words of Institution as the indispensable absolute for a valid sacrament. If the use of the *verba* (or the Epiclesis, for that matter) should prove to be the one thing, among all the others, that proves indispensable, then one might also argue that everything else might conceivably be dispensed with as long as this one thing is in place. In other words, the minimum necessary might be understood to be the *only* thing really necessary. This move toward the minimum no doubt played a role in the reduction of classic eucharistic prayer in the Lutheran and Reformed liturgies of the Reformation era, a reduction that continues to affect us even in the twenty-first century, as the Words of Institution are not infrequently understood to be the only words necessary for the sacrament.

3

Eucharistic Prayer
and the Reformation

Whenever the church finds itself in a time of crisis or of cultural transition, everything comes under review, including its worship. We are in such a time now, and it is evident that there are pressures and cross-pressures as the church tries to re-form its worship in ways appropriate to the times while keeping faith with its past. The sixteenth century was also a time of deep cultural change, most familiar to us, perhaps, in the dynamics that gave birth to the Protestant Reformation. The Reformation was not only about the nature of authority in the church, or the role of Scripture, or the proper formulation of doctrine. It also had to do with worship.

The way a community worships reveals its basic theological commitments. It is foolish to believe that theology matters but that the details of worship do not matter. The details of worship not only express an implicit theology, but they also influence worshippers by forming them, however inarticulately, in the same theological presuppositions. When the medieval priest said Mass every Sunday (or even every day), but co-opted all the parts of the service for himself without any participation by anyone else, including the congregation, his action in worship both expressed a theology and imprinted that theology upon those who experienced it. When he prayed the Canon at every mass, but in a foreign language and, for the most part, in a hushed voice, his action expressed a theology and silently advocated the same theology to those present. When the priest blessed bread and wine, but consumed it all alone, without a congregation; or when members of the congregation communed but were denied the cup, those actions and omissions made a theological statement that spoke more loudly than any official theology.

CRITIQUING THEOLOGY BY CRITIQUING PRACTICE

The Reformers understood that it was not possible to critique or challenge the prevailing theology as doctrine without also critiquing and challenging that theology as it took form in practice, including, most especially, in worship. When it came to the Eucharist, Martin Luther, John Calvin, and most of Calvin's reforming allies agreed that the Lord's Supper was meant to be celebrated weekly in a service of both Word and Sacrament. Eventually, the Reformers created services in the vernacular. They provided published forms for the service, and all prayer at the Lord's Supper was offered clearly and audibly, so that the congregation could follow and understand. They brushed aside the many and varied allegorical interpretations of the eucharistic action, and pruned the gestures and ceremonies that supposedly mimicked events in the life and death of Christ. By setting the Lord's Supper next to the reading and preaching of the Word, they linked it as clearly as they could to the gospel promises.

The Reformers insisted that the Eucharist was not a private act, but that it was both by and for the whole gathered assembly. The Supper was not celebrated without communicants. Virtually the whole congregation ate and drank together. In these reforms, the leaders of the Reformation attempted to express a theological vision that was in some ways coherent with and in other ways different from the official theology of the papal church.

In both the Lutheran and Genevan Reformations, the chief Reformers critiqued the medieval doctrine of the Mass as a sacrifice. The theme of sacrifice, in their view, had become so dominating and so distorting that they repudiated it vigorously. In Geneva, this distancing from the notion of sacrifice and the desire to recover a sense of the Eucharist as a meal, led to the renaming of the medieval altar as the communion table.[1]

CONTINUITY AND DISCONTINUITY

However, even as the Reformers distanced themselves from a eucharistic theology that seemed to suggest a repetition of Christ's once-for-all sacrifice, they imported into their own liturgical systems the medieval church's accent on the suffering and death of the Lord. The themes of atonement, sacrifice for sin, and the subsequent need for penitence dominated their Eucharists, escaping close scrutiny by the Reformers, thus managing to persist in the churches of the Reformation without challenge. Their conception of the Eucharist as primarily a re-presentation of the Lord's *Last* Supper contributed to the failure of their hope to restore the broken relationship between Word and Sacrament by recovering both preaching and a weekly Communion. The tone of melancholy, penitence, and humiliation was not something a congregation was eager to bear every Lord's Day.

In matters of worship, Luther was less radical than Calvin and more willing to include in his service forms inherited from the pre-Reformation church. However, in one particular he was adamant. Both in his Latin *Formula Missae* and in his *Deutsche Messe*, he was determined to remove all suggestion of a eucharistic sacrifice. The *German Mass*, prepared when Luther had grown bold enough to move beyond his reformed version of the Latin Mass, ended the eucharistic prayer at the Sanctus. Nothing of the traditional prayer remained except for the Preface (the first part of the thanksgiving) and the Words of Institution. And why not? If, as was commonly accepted in the medieval church, the Words of Institution were the only part of the Canon that was absolutely essential (for the consecration of the bread and wine), then what rationale might there be for retaining the traditional eucharistic prayer(s), so steeped in the language of sacrifice?

Even into the late twentieth century, some Lutheran liturgies followed Luther's own practice, which had been at the same time both conservative and radical. The 1958 Lutheran *Service Book and Hymnal* offered the option of eucharistic prayer after the fashion of Luther, consisting only of a Preface, Sanctus, and Words of Institution, followed by the Lord's Prayer, although a tripartite, or Trinitarian, form of the prayer was the preferred option.[2] The same options, including the truncated form, continue to be offered in the 1978 *Lutheran Book of Worship*.[3]

THE "ESSENTIALS" OF THE EUCHARISTIC PRAYER

It's a matter of curiosity that both Lutheran and Reformed churches give the impression in practice, if not in theory, that the Words of Institution are indispensable in celebrating the Lord's Supper, while practices of eucharistic praying that developed from as early as we have any record have been laid aside. Protestants would probably be surprised to consider to what extent their traditions have been shaped by the very pre-Reformation milieu from which they imagine they have distanced themselves.

From very early on, the churches of the East included in their eucharistic prayers petitions for the Holy Spirit to bless the assembly and the gifts of bread and wine. They did so, at first, without any systematic theory about a change in the bread and wine, but their theology did not permit them to omit prayer for the Holy Spirit. The Roman church's eucharistic prayer, on the other hand, included no explicit prayer for the Holy Spirit, but considered the Words of

Institution as the absolute minimum necessary for an act of consecration to take place. Developments in East and West, then, led to two distinct traditions, one focusing on the Epiclesis, the other on the Words of Institution. The Roman tradition, more inclined to think in legal terms, could conceive that a "valid" consecration was possible if at least the Words of Institution were used. Whenever a necessary minimum is declared, the natural tendency of human beings is to move toward the minimum. Presbyterians, Lutherans, and other Protestants have done exactly that when they reduce the "essentials" of eucharistic prayer to the Words of Institution. Presbyterians may find themselves dismayed when visiting services of denominations that omit even those, but once we conceive the eucharistic actions in terms of minimums, it should come as no surprise that some will discover a minimum even more reduced than our own.

CALVIN'S REFORMED PREDECESSORS IN STRASBOURG

When Presbyterians think of the Reformation, they are inclined to begin with John Calvin. Certainly Calvin was the most influential of those who shaped what came to be the Reformed tradition, but he was not the first. The city of Strasbourg was the site of reforming activity preceding Calvin, and he enjoyed the hospitality of that city from 1538 to 1541, during the years of his exile from Geneva. Although a German-speaking city, a number of French-speaking residents lived there. While banished from Geneva, Calvin became pastor of the French Reformed congregation in Strasbourg.

Martin Bucer was the chief reformer in Strasbourg, although he was joined by a number of talented leaders. As early as 1524, a man named Diebold Schwartz had created a German vernacular version of the Mass, called *Die Teutsche Messe*, which closely resembles the traditional Roman Canon. Bucer revised Schwartz's work more than once, beginning as early as 1525. Bucer's revision provided three forms for the eucharistic prayer. Calvin respected Bucer and learned from him, and in fact adopted the third form of Bucer's eucharistic prayer as his own with only slight variations. (For a time line of Reformed liturgies, see Appendix I.)

All of Bucer's eucharistic prayers are included within pastoral prayers or intercessions, pivoting around the themes of depravity, sin, and the need for forgiveness. (See Appendix A.) The eucharistic section has a kind of Anamnesis and a plea to God that the people "may now receive this, his goodness and gift, and with true faith now partake of his true body and true blood—indeed be himself, our Savior, true God and true man, the only real bread of heaven."[4] In a sort of indirection, this portion of the prayer functions as a quasi-Epiclesis much as the Quam oblationem does in the Roman Canon. Bucer ended his eucharistic liturgy with the Lord's Prayer, as do most of the ancient liturgies. He did not include the Words of Institution within the prayer, as they always had been placed since their first documented use, but located them immediately before the distribution of the bread and cup.[5]

One finds in Bucer's liturgy what some have called "the Reformed Sursum Corda" ("Lift up your hearts"), drawn from Colossians 3:1.[6] It does not take the traditional form of a dialogue between the presiding minister and the people, but resembles a kind of exhortation: "Therefore lift your hearts on high, seeking the heavenly things in heaven, where Jesus Christ is sitting at the right hand of the father."[7]

This lifting of hearts on high plays an important role in Reformed eucharistic theology as it developed in Calvin. Disputes among various Reformers, with Luther and Zwingli at opposite ends of the spectrum, had to do with whether Jesus Christ was in fact present in the sacrament, and if so, where. Luther asserted the doctrine of ubiquity, that is, that the risen, ascended Christ was present everywhere, and that his human and divine natures could not be separated, so that, in the Eucharist, Christ became bodily as well as spiritually present in, with, and under the species of bread and wine. Calvin was closer to Luther than to Zwingli, for whom Christ was present only in memory, yet Calvin was reluctant to locate Christ bodily in the bread and wine. His argument, which may seem naive today, was that, after the ascension, Christ was seated at the right hand of the Father. In the Eucharist, Christ does not come down to us, but by the power of the Holy Spirit we ascend to him. The argument as Calvin framed it to argue against Luther's doctrine of ubiquity is naive; however, in our day, instructed perhaps by Paul Ricoeur's image of a "second naiveté," it works as metaphor. Of particular interest is that some Orthodox theologians use very similar language.[8]

Some of Calvin's reforming predecessors influenced the form of his liturgy, including prayer at the Eucharist. Oecolampadius, the reformer of Basel, created a rite in 1525. Guillaume Farel, the first-generation Genevan reformer who had recruited Calvin to take the lead in that city, produced a liturgy for Neuchâtel and Geneva in 1533, drawing upon liturgies from Basel, Bern, and Strasbourg.

CALVIN'S RITE

Although Calvin suggested an order of service in the 1536 edition of the *Institutes*,[9] he created a somewhat different rite after his sojourn in Strasbourg.[10]

Calvin drew upon what he had already written in the *Institutes* and from the liturgies of Oecolampadius and Farel. He created another revision in 1547, the Genevan Liturgy,[11] which was in fact an abbreviated form of Bucer's Strasbourg Liturgy, which is the true parent liturgy of the Reformed tradition.[12]

Calvin added to the eucharistic liturgy he had received from Bucer a long exhortation, drawn in large part from Farel's liturgy. (See Appendix B.) Like Bucer, Calvin did not include the Words of Institution within the eucharistic prayer, but unlike Bucer, he placed them at the beginning of the exhortation rather than at the distribution. In that position, they serve as a warrant, declaring by what authority the church celebrates the Lord's Supper. For Calvin, use of the Words of Institution was invariable. He took as the indispensable minimum what the Roman church had likewise taken.

The irony is that although Calvin understood the Lord's Supper to be an occasion for thanksgiving, in his rite the theme of thanksgiving is peripheral and muted.[13] In the Genevan Liturgy, on days when the Lord's Supper was to be celebrated, the presiding minister added to the usual prayers after the sermon an additional prayer directly related to the Supper, in which he prayed, "Thus may we render *praise and thanks* unto thee without ceasing"[14] (italics added). However, no other note of thanksgiving was sounded, although *after* the people had communed, the service concluded with a prayer that begins, "Heavenly Father, we offer thee eternal praise and thanks that thou hast granted so great a benefit to us poor sinners."[15]

ZWINGLI AND OTHER REFORMERS

It would not do to bypass Huldrych Zwingli, the reformer of Zurich, whose eucharistic theology staked out a position as far removed as possible from the pre-Reformation church. In 1525, he created his own rite for the Lord's Supper, tellingly called *Action or Use of the Lord's Supper: A Memorial or Thanksgiving of Christ As It Will Be Begun in Zurich at Easter in the Year 1525*. If used at all, it was used only briefly. The Zurich Liturgy includes such traditional liturgical material as the Gloria in excelsis, and involves a good deal of dialogue between pastor and people, along with antiphonal voices alternating between men and women. Although there is prayer in this service, there is no eucharistic prayer, which is appropriate to Zwingli's theology, since the bread and wine serve chiefly as reminders of Christ's redemptive work and not as a means by which the risen Christ becomes present to the assembly. The presider at the Lord's Supper is not the pastor, but one designated as "Server." The order is very simple.

Zwingli's Liturgy of the Lord's Supper
Exhortation
Lord's Prayer (kneeling)
Prayer for Worthy Reception
Words of Institution
Distribution
Psalm 112

Zwingli's liturgy is not without elements of thanksgiving, perhaps even more vivid than in Calvin's liturgy. In a Preface to be read by the pastor early in the service leading to Communion, Zwingli described the sacrament as "a thanksgiving and a rejoicing before Almighty God for the goodness which He has shown us through his Son."[16]

Although John Knox seems to be an exception, the tradition of Farel, Oecolampadius, and Bucer, as it culminated in Calvin's Genevan Liturgy, radically alters the ancient and venerable traditions of eucharistic prayer. Even Luther, as conservative as he was in liturgical matters, radically pruned the Canon of the Mass, leaving only a portion of the ancient prayers. How do we explain the disconnect between the high eucharistic theology of Calvin and the barrenness of what passes for eucharistic prayer in his liturgy?

CALVIN'S RITE VERSUS HIS THEOLOGY OF THE EUCHARIST

The lack of connection between theology and practice may be partially explained simply by reference to the times. Calvin and others among the Reformers felt the need to distance themselves from Roman doctrine, which was embedded in Roman practice. Neither Luther nor Calvin was comfortable with the prevailing interpretation of the Mass as a sacrifice, particularly as the doctrine was popularly explained. Calvin could speak of a sacrifice of praise and thanksgiving, but he and the other Reformers took a firm stand on biblical grounds that Christ's sacrifice on the cross for our redemption was once and for all. It was not only impossible to repeat the sacrifice but desperately presumptuous even to suggest that such a thing was happening in the Mass.[17] The very fact that Mass was offered daily and often even simultaneously at multiple altars in the same churches for various intentions of those sponsoring them with their offerings contributed to the perception that Christ was being sacrificed again and again. Of course, the more sophisticated Catholic theologians could and did interpret sacrifice in more acceptable terms, but as long as they had not had to confront theological adversaries, it had not been necessary for them to restrain and qualify the popular conceptions.

The idea of a sacrifice being re-presented in every eucharist seemed linked to the doctrine of transubstantiation, that is, a supernatural and metaphysical change in the essential nature of the bread and wine. Transubstantiation, in turn, depended on the idea of "consecration," which in the Roman Canon was believed to occur when the Words of Institution were said within the prayer. That may explain why Calvin and his school pulled the Words of Institution out of the prayer and used them either before or after it.

Bryan Spinks suggests that Calvin had understood Jesus' own thanksgiving at the Last Supper to be addressed not to God, but to the disciples, in order to draw their attention to "so lofty a mystery."[18] While the institution narrative itself certainly was addressed to the disciples, Jesus' prayer was not. Calvin, if he in fact took the view that Jesus' prayer at the Supper was essentially didactic, was mistaken. As a Jew, Jesus prayed to bless God, thank God for particular circumstances, and petition God; but certainly not in order to speak to God so that his disciples might overhear it and learn a lesson in theology.

If Spinks is correct in his understanding of Calvin, Calvin framed his own prayer to emphasize the gravity of the sacrament for the benefit of the congregation. If Jesus' prayer had been the equivalent of an exhortation to those who overheard it, then Calvin's prayer served the same purpose. Calvin's prayer, which, on Sundays when they celebrated the Lord's Supper, was added to a long pastoral prayer that followed the sermon every Sunday, reads as though it were instruction and exhortation addressed to the congregation.

It is *after* this pastoral prayer that Calvin's eucharistic service moves to the Words of Institution used as a warrant at the beginning of the eucharistic liturgy, then segues into a lengthy warning that serves to excommunicate those who are not worthy to commune. An exhortation ends with the Reformed Sursum Corda: "Let us lift our spirits and hearts on high where Jesus Christ is in the glory of His Father."[19]

THE CONTINUING INFLUENCE OF MEDIEVAL PIETY

The tone of the Genevan eucharistic service, hedged around with solemn warnings, tends to accent the penitential at the expense of thanksgiving. This, in fact, is not so terribly different from the tone of the pre-Reformation Roman Mass. Calvin had inherited from the piety of the medieval church a very sober, grave understanding of the Eucharist, interpreted primarily in terms of Christ's *Last* Supper, with little or no attention to the themes of resurrection or eating and drinking with the risen Lord. The resurrection themes, present in Scripture (e.g., Luke 24, John 21) and prominent in the eucharistic celebrations of the early centuries of the church, had been obscured in the medieval eucharistic celebration and continued to be eclipsed in the Reformed rites.

One can understand, perhaps, how Calvin shaped his eucharistic rite as he did, since he was so determined to form a disciplined community that understood its own rites with as much clarity and lack of ambiguity as possible. Nevertheless, Calvin's eucharistic liturgy is not devoted to praise or thanksgiving, and it seems to turn the prayer inside out, giving the impression of being directed more *to* the congregation than *from* the congregation *to* God.

Although Calvin was acquainted with the Fathers of the early church, he did not follow their example when it came to eucharistic prayer.[20] Of course, a priority he shared with other Reformers was that worshippers *understand* the sacrament in order to partake worthily. Against the background of the medieval church, whose rites seemed to the people to be akin to magic, Calvin initiated a program of clarification. He was determined, for example, to restore the dignity and power of the Word, both by reading Scripture in the vernacular language and by preaching from the biblical text. The Word illuminated the meaning of the Sacrament, and the Sacrament sealed the Word.

The old rites and ceremonies had accumulated a plethora of gestures and symbolic actions, none of which communicated its own meaning unambiguously, and each one requiring to be explained allegorically and explained differently by various interpreters. For Calvin, simplicity led to understanding, but, in practice, the supreme importance of the liturgy being understood led him (and his successors) to a didacticism that ran the risk of disfiguring and even inhibiting true prayerfulness. The urgency of Calvin's reforming agenda and the need to rebut current Roman Catholic practice may have led to his misreading of the role of prayer both in Jewish meal practice (e.g., the Last Supper) and in the Eucharist of the early church.

INFLUENCE OF EASTERN ORTHODOX EUCHARISTIC THEOLOGY

Paradoxically, it would seem that Calvin's eucharistic theology would have led quite naturally to eucharistic prayer on a model similar to that of the Eastern churches. His theology of the sacrament is more reminiscent of Orthodox theology than that of the Roman church. The strongest link is in Calvin's thought about the role of the Holy Spirit. Calvin rejected the notion of the Zwinglians that when we receive Christ by faith, we receive him only by the understanding and the imagination. It was by the Holy Spirit that "all that Christ himself is and has is conveyed to us."[21]

Other Reformation-era Reformed confessions affirm the same theology, derived from Calvin. For example, the Scots Confession of 1560 says that this union and conjunction which we have with the body and blood of Christ Jesus in the right use of the sacraments "is wrought by means of the Holy Ghost."[22]

The Orthodox, unlike the Roman church, did not attempt to spell out their eucharistic theology in precise philosophical or metaphysical terms. The Orthodox strongly affirmed Christ's real presence in the Eucharist, and even spoke of a "change" occurring in the course of the eucharistic liturgy, though without defining the nature of that change.[23] However, they laid heavy emphasis on the action of the Holy Spirit in delivering Jesus Christ to his church (in a sacramental way), which the Reformed confessions echo. In fact, according to Max Thurian, Calvin derived his theology of the Holy Spirit in the Eucharist from a sermon attributed to John Chrysostom.[24]

The Roman church did not place such emphasis on the Holy Spirit in the sacrament, and there is no explicit appeal for the Spirit (no Epiclesis) in the Roman Canon, except perhaps if one accepts the argument that the Quam oblationem serves the purpose. Calvin's theology clearly departs from familiar Western precedents and exhibits a kinship with the Eastern churches, which makes it even more a matter of curiosity that his theology has not shaped his manner of eucharistic prayer. It would have been reasonable to expect some sort of Epiclesis, at the very least, in his prayer at the Table. The best explanation for the omission would seem to be that, as Spinks alleges, Calvin may have thought of the prayer in didactic terms, as though offered for the sake of those who heard it, instructing the people in the duty of praise, thanksgiving, and petition more effectively than actually doing those things.

For example, Calvin criticized the practice of the priest praying the Canon sotto voce, out of the hearing of the people. Among several good reasons for being critical of such a practice, one important one was that the Words of Institution, included in the Canon, were therefore not heard by the congregation.

> Hence . . . arose this error: they did not observe that those promises by which consecration is accomplished are directed not to the elements themselves but to those who receive them. Certainly Christ does not say to the bread that it shall become his body, but he commands his disciples to eat and promises them participation in his body and blood.[25]

In other words, Calvin seems to say that "consecration" is accomplished by a reiteration of the "promises" represented in the Words of Institution addressed to the congregation. They mean nothing if not actually heard by the people. He adds,

> Here we should not imagine some magic incantation, supposing it enough to have mumbled the words, as if they were to be heard by the elements; but let us understand that these words are living preaching which edifies its hearers, penetrates into their very minds, impresses itself upon their hearts and settles there, and reveals its effectiveness in the fulfillment of what it promises.[26]

Although Calvin frequently identified the Word to mean preaching, in this case, when he uses the words "living preaching," Calvin seems to be referring to the Words of Institution, for in the same section of the *Institutes* he criticizes taking the sacrament to the sick "without a recital of Christ's institution." The better practice, he argues, would be to "join with the sign the true explanation of the mystery." "Silence involves abuse and fault. If the promises are recited and the mystery declared, so that they who are about to receive it may receive it with benefit, there is no reason to doubt that this is *a true consecration*"[27] (italics added). Although Calvin finds the preaching of the Word, with its promises, to be essential to the right celebration of the Eucharist, it would seem that the Words of Institution, with their promises, might serve in place of preaching if the situation required it. The *verba* might be only a bare minimum, but even that role grants to them an importance exceeding that of any particular form of prayer. Calvin's line of reasoning leads, ironically and perhaps unintentionally, to identifying the Words of Institution as possessing the same crucial degree of importance as they occupied in traditional Roman Catholic doctrine, though for different reasons, while Calvin's theology of the Holy Spirit's role in making the sacrament becomes implicit, rather than explicit, in his liturgy.

While not related to the formation of Calvin's liturgy, other streams of the Reformed tradition linked "consecration" to the Word, even while affirming a sacramental theology linked to the Spirit. Heinrich Bullinger's Second Helvetic Confession (1561) affirms, in a quite orthodox manner, that it is Christ Himself who is given in the sacraments, but liturgically, the accent falls on Word rather than Spirit.

> For they [sacraments] are consecrated by the Word, and shown to be sanctified by him who instituted them. . . . But when the Word of God is added to them, together with invocation of the divine name, and the renewing of their first institution and sanctification, then these signs are consecrated, and shown to be sanctified by Christ. For Christ's first institution and consecration of the Sacraments remains always effectual in the Church of God. . . . And hence in the celebration of the Sacraments the very words of Christ are repeated.[28]

No doubt both Calvin and Bullinger understood the Spirit to be at work in and through the Word (whether meaning the Word preached or the Words of Institution used as a warrant explicitly linked to the eucharistic action), so Calvin does not deny his own theology in his eucharistic liturgy, even though he has not taken care to make it explicit.

As a layperson, Calvin had never offered the eucharistic prayer of the Roman church, nor even heard it prayed aloud. However, the various medieval manuals, with their allegorical interpretations of the Mass centered on Christ's passion, and the individualistic and penitential piety that characterized the devotions meant to occupy the congregation while the incomprehensible "sacrifice" proceeded, would likely have served to alienate him from the texts that comprised the prayers of the Canon. What is remarkable is that John Knox came so much closer to true eucharistic prayer than his mentor.

INFLUENCE OF THE GENEVAN LITURGY ON LITURGIES IN ENGLISH

Calvin's Genevan Liturgy exercised enormous influence among Reformed churches both on the Continent and in England. William Huycke translated it into English in 1550, and John Knox in 1556 for the English congregation in Geneva, although Knox altered the prayers at the table. Though Knox's *Book of Common Order* of 1564 derived from Calvin's liturgy, it contained a new eucharistic prayer, which is much more eucharistic in tone than Calvin's.[29] (See Appendix D.) Following Calvin's practice, the minister reads the Words of Institution (1 Cor. 11) as a warrant before a lengthy exhortation. The exhortation ends with a Reformed Sursum Corda ("let us lift up our minds by faith"), after which follows the prayer. The eucharistic prayer itself follows the form neither of the Roman Canon nor of the Eastern anaphoras, but it does include elements traditionally associated with prayer at the Eucharist. The prayer begins with lengthy praise, including praise of God for the creation of human beings in God's own image, and adds praise for our redemption in Christ, mentioning his death, resurrection, and coming again. The prayer includes an eschatological reference and concludes with a Trinitarian doxology.[30] Although there is no Epiclesis in the printed order, Celtic practice from even before the Reformation included prayer for the Holy Spirit in the eucharistic prayer, and some ministers supplied their own.[31]

Anglicans do not ordinarily consider themselves "Reformed," but there was, nevertheless, a good deal of Genevan influence on the Church of England in the early years after the Reformation, as well as the direct influence of Calvin's mentor, Martin Bucer, who had fled to England in 1549. Conflicts involving Scottish Presbyterians and Episcopalians, and English Anglicans, Presbyterians, and Congregationalists also left impressions here and there on Anglican worship. In the Church of England, the eucharistic prayer in the first Book of Common Prayer (1549) was simply a vernacular reworking of the pre-Reformation Roman Canon. Theologically, it was deliberately ambiguous. It differs from subsequent versions (1552 on) of the English BCP in that it made use of an explicit Epiclesis. Some scholars believe that Cranmer was deliberately borrowing from Eastern sources, but it is more likely that his Epiclesis was simply his own version of the Roman Canon's Quam oblationem, which includes the petition that "this offering" may "become for us the body and blood of your most beloved Son, our Lord Jesus Christ." The Epiclesis in the 1549 BCP includes an appeal for God to work through the Word as well as the Spirit, praying to the Father,

> with thy holy spirite and worde, vouchsafe to blesse and sanctifie these thy gyftes, and creatures of bread and wyne, that they maie be unto us the bodye and bloude of thy moste derely beloved sonne Jesus Christe."[32]

In the subsequent revision of 1552, Cranmer, whose Zwinglian orientation had become less guarded, dropped the Epiclesis, as well as a formal Anamnesis, probably because they seemed to suggest some sort of metaphysical change in the elements, as in the Roman doctrine of transubstantiation.

SCOTTISH, ENGLISH, AND AMERICAN EUCHARISTIC PRAYERS

The American Book of Common Prayer, unlike the English version after 1549, has always included an Epiclesis. The reason for the difference is that the American version of the BCP stems from Scottish sources. For about half of the seventeenth century, there was little difference between Scottish Presbyterian and Scottish Episcopal worship. When the Scottish Episcopal Church created its own BCP in 1764, it made use of a 1637 revision of the BCP that had been authorized by the king with the intention of winning Scottish Presbyterian approval of a prayer book closely resembling the English book. The 1637 book made a number of concessions to Scottish practice and sensibilities. This book was met by a riot, led by Jenny Geddes, when it was introduced at St. Giles in Edinburgh. Although the riot may have been planned rather than spontaneous, it was directed not against the use of a book (the Scots had long been accustomed to Knox's *Book of Common Order*), but to the fact that this was, to their way of thinking, an *English* book, imposed by English authority.

The 1637 liturgy, popularly, but inaccurately, called "Laud's Liturgy," after
the incumbent archbishop of Canterbury, incorporates the Scottish practice
of including an Epiclesis, even though no explicit invocation of the Spirit had
been provided in the published form composed by Knox for his *Book of Common
Order*. This inclusion makes explicit what had, according to spokespersons
of the time, been a persistent, but unofficial, practice, as noted above.[33] The
origins of the practice are obscure, but it is likely that the pre-Reformation
Celtic church included an Epiclesis in its eucharistic prayer. The so-called
Gallic, or Gallican, liturgies included a specifically Celtic subspecies in use
among the peoples of northwestern Europe, but most especially the Irish and
the Scots. One of the peculiarities of the Gallican liturgies in general was that
they made use of various sources, including Eastern materials, and most particularly, an explicit Epiclesis. Although all the Gallican liturgies finally gave
way to the Roman Canon, it may be that Scottish practice both before and
after the Reformation represented the survival of certain aspects of the old
Celtic eucharistic tradition.[34] In any case, despite its unofficial status, the use
of the Epiclesis was apparently important enough to the Scots that they
pressed it upon King Charles I, who conceded to them in this matter, even
though inclusion of an Epiclesis in the liturgy of 1637 did not conform to
English practice.

The eucharistic prayer in the 1637 revision of the BCP does not follow the
tripartite Antiochene form, though it includes most of the material traditionally found in classic eucharistic prayers. It begins with the traditional opening
dialogue, followed by a Proper Preface and Sanctus. The section of the prayer
immediately following the Sanctus recalls the sacrifice of Christ, and functions
as a kind of warrant for the sacrament. This section includes the Epiclesis,
which is almost identical to that in Cranmer's 1549 version of the BCP (see
earlier in this book, p. 35):

> Hear us, O merciful Father, we most humbly beseech thee, and of thy
> Almighty goodness vouchsafe so to bless and sanctify with thy word
> and Holy Spirit these thy gifts and creatures of bread and wine, that
> they may be unto us the body and blood of thy most dearly beloved
> Son.[35]

The linking of "thy word and Holy Spirit" (reflecting usage in Cranmer's 1549
BCP) seems to represent an attention to Reformed sensibilities as well as being
reminiscent, though probably not intentionally, of some eucharistic prayers
from early centuries in which the Epiclesis is worded such as to call upon the
logos rather than the Holy Spirit.[36]

By contrast, the English prayer book dating from 1662 has no Epiclesis, going directly from "we most humbly beseech thee" to "and grant that we receiving these thy Creatures of Bread and Wine . . . may be partakers of his most blessed body and blood," followed by the Words of Institution.[37] Although the 1637 prayer book had been rejected in Scotland, primarily for political reasons, the Scottish Episcopal rite of 1764 made use of it, and it became one source for the American Episcopal Book of Common Prayer, beginning with the first American rite of 1790.[38]

The Scottish prayer of 1637, like the 1549 BCP and the Roman Quam oblationem, locates the Epiclesis *before* the Words of Institution (and manual acts), which precede a kind of Anamnesis, recalling Christ's "blessed passion, mighty resurrection, and glorious ascension" with thanksgiving, and a petition that the Father might accept the "sacrifice of praise and thanksgiving" and that "we and all thy whole Church may obtain remission of our sins, and all other benefits of his passion." The Scottish prayer continues with an oblation and concludes with a Trinitarian doxology and the Lord's Prayer.

The American prayer book, following the example of the Scottish Episcopal BCP of 1764, positions its Epiclesis differently from the 1637 book, introducing the Epiclesis *after* the Words of Institution, in the Antiochene position, though *preceding* rather than following an Anamnesis. The placement of the Epiclesis is the same as the Nonjurors' Liturgy of 1718. The Nonjurors were those who in 1689 refused to take the oath of allegiance to King William and Queen Mary.[39] The first American Episcopal bishop, Samuel Seabury, was consecrated by Nonjuring Episcopalians in Scotland, and through him the Nonjurors' Liturgy exercised an influence on the shaping of the eucharistic prayer in the American version of the Book of Common Prayer, accounting for the fact that the American version of the BCP has an Epiclesis, while the English BCP (1662) does not. Thus the American prayer book derives in large part from influences originating in Scottish Presbyterian and Episcopal practice and sensibilities, particularly in the use of an Epiclesis in its eucharistic prayer, the wording of which closely follows that of Laud's Liturgy of 1637, derived from the BCP of 1549. This is the text from the American version of the BCP (cf. 1637, p. 36):

> And we most humbly beseech thee, O merciful Father, to hear us; and, of thy almighty goodness, vouchsafe to bless and sanctify, with thy word and Holy Spirit, these thy gifts and creatures of bread and wine; that we, receiving them according to thy Son our Savior Jesus Christ's holy institution, in remembrance of his Death and Passion, may be partakers of his most blessed Body and Blood.[40]

The American version closely resembles the Antiochene order.

Laud's Liturgy, 1637	English BCP, 1662	Nonjurors' Liturgy of 1718	American BCP 1790–1979
Opening Dialogue	Opening Dialogue	Opening Dialogue	Opening Dialogue
"It is very meet . . ."	"It is meet . . ."	"It is very meet . . ."	"It is very meet . . ."
Proper Preface	Proper Preface	Sanctus and Benedictus	Proper Preface
Sanctus	Sanctus	Proper Preface and Anamnesis	Sanctus
Epiclesis	Prayer of Humble Access	*Verba*	Prayer of Humble Access
Anamnesis with *Verba*	Anamnesis with *Verba*	Manual Acts	Anamnesis with *Verba* and
and Manual Acts	and Manual Acts	Anamnesis continues	Manual Acts
Oblation	Distribution	Oblation	Epiclesis
Lord's Prayer	Lord's Prayer	Epiclesis	Oblation
Prayer of Humble Access	Oblation	Intercessions	Distribution
Distribution		Memorial of the faithful departed	Lord's Prayer
		Great Amen	
		Lord's Prayer	
		The Peace	
		Invitation*	
		Confession and Absolution	
		Prayer of Humble Access	
		Distribution	

*In the other books, the Invitation, Confession, and Absolution precede the Opening Dialogue.

It is a matter of curiosity that the 1637 Scottish book permits the use of the Words of Institution alone when additional consecration is necessary, particularly since such practice is contrary to the usage of Knox's *Book of Common Order* and seems also to be inconsistent with Scottish preferences, since it had been so important to the Scots to add an Epiclesis in this revision. This follows Anglican precedent, since in England, ordinary practice was to use only the Words of Institution when additional consecration was required.[41]

THE WESTMINSTER DIRECTORY FOR WORSHIP

It is a source of great fascination that the first Westminster Directory for Worship in 1644 followed Knox's *Book of Common Order* more closely than it did Genevan models, and even went beyond Knox in its specific prescriptions for eucharistic prayer. (See Appendix F.) The Scots did not prevail in many matters at Westminster, but they did manage to persuade the English Puritans that the Directory needed to provide for a "fuller" Prayer of Thanksgiving than either the Book of Common Prayer or the *Book of Common Order*.[42] The resulting Westminster Directory offered a suggested outline for the eucharistic prayer, including thanksgiving, an Anamnesis and an Epiclesis. In the tradition of Calvin, the Directory declares that the elements will be "set apart and sanctified to this holy use, *by the Word of Institution and Prayer*"[43] (italics added). Although the Directory is, for the most part, a set of rubrics rather than texts, in the case of the Eucharist it provides prayers that might be used word for word, although introduced by the qualifying statement, "Let the Prayer, Thanksgiving, or Blessing of the Bread and Wine, be to this effect:"[44] The order for "the Celebration of the Communion, or Sacrament of the Lord's Supper" states:

Westminster Directory
Exhortation
Setting Apart of the Bread and Wine
Words of Institution (1 Corinthians 11)
Tripartite Prayer
    Thanksgiving
    Profession of Faith in Jesus Christ (Anamnesis)
    Epiclesis
Manual Acts (Fraction, Lifting of the Cup)
Distribution

The recommendations regarding the Epiclesis are particularly striking. The Directory urges the church

> earnestly to pray to God, the Father of all mercies, and God of all con-solation, to vouchsafe His gracious presence, and the effectual work-ing of His Spirit in us; and so to sanctify these Elements both of Bread and Wine, and so to bless His own Ordinance, that we may receive by faith the Body and Blood of Jesus Christ, crucified for us, and so to feed upon Him, that He may be made one with us, and we one with Him; that He may live in us, and we in Him, and to Him who hath loved us, and given Himself for us.[45]

The Epiclesis is strikingly similar to that in the 1637 Scottish version of the Book of Common Prayer (the so-called Laud's Liturgy), though omitting any mention of the "Word" alongside the "Spirit."

PURITAN INFLUENCE

Puritans, of course, differed from one another along a spectrum from those who wished to remain in the established Church of England to those who were determined to find purity by separating from it. After the restoration of the monarchy, King Charles II called the Savoy Conference of 1661 in hopes of creating a revision of the Book of Common Prayer that would prove accept-able to both Episcopalians and Puritans. The only Puritans present at the Savoy Conference were Presbyterians. The Independents—later Congrega-tionalists—had no part in it. The Puritans presented to the conference a list of "Exceptions" to the English prayer book and suggestions for amendments. One suggested amendment was that "in the 'Prayer of Consecration' a peti-tion for consecration and directions for the fraction were to be added."[46] The "petition for consecration" refers to an explicit Epiclesis. The fraction (the so-called "manual acts"—the breaking of the bread) played a significant role in the Reformed understanding of the meaning of the sacrament as expressed in the sacramental actions.

The call to the Savoy Conference included the proposal that the members be invited to supply alternative forms in scriptural phrasing. The Puritan side assigned Richard Baxter, a Presbyterian, to provide such forms, and the result was his "Reformed Liturgy."

Eucharistic Prayer in Baxter's Reformed Liturgy of 1661
Prayer to the Father for sanctification of the elements
"Sanctify these thy creatures of bread and wine . . ."

Words of Institution

Ministerial declaration of consecration

> "This bread and wine, being set apart, and consecrated to this holy use by God's appointment, are now no common bread and wine, but sacramentally the body and blood of Christ."

Prayer to the Son

Breaking of the Bread, Pouring of the Cup

Prayer to the Spirit for illumination

> "Most Holy Spirit . . . illuminate us, that by faith we may see him that is here represented to us."

Distribution[47]

The Lord's Prayer does not appear in the eucharistic prayer because it would have been offered during the prayers preceding the sermon (in the placement of the prayers, the Independents at the Westminster Assembly had prevailed over Presbyterian practice, the Presbyterians having heretofore followed the custom of Calvin and Knox in offering the "Long Prayer" after, rather than before, the sermon).

From the middle of the seventeenth century to the opening of the nineteenth, we have no printed liturgies to detail the patterns of prayer in the free-church traditions derived from Puritanism. However, observers have recorded general observations of such prayers among the Independents (later Congregationalists). Generally, the minister offered separate prayers over the bread and the wine. The form of the prayer, in some cases, more or less followed the prescriptions of the Westminster Directory. Apparently there was a sense that the bread and wine required "consecration," achieved by the use of the Words of Institution, thanksgiving framed in the minister's own words, and the fraction and libation (breaking and pouring).[48] Eucharistic theology sometimes followed Calvin and quite frequently Zwingli. Since much was left to the discretion of the minister, it is likely that practices varied widely.

In the century following the Westminster Assembly and the adoption of its Directory by the Church of Scotland, the English Puritan movement in its more extreme forms profoundly influenced the worship of the Scottish kirk. Some on the Puritan left rejected all set forms, whether from Canterbury or from Geneva. This was quite different from Reformed churches on the Continent, where set forms were common. In England, such rejection might be traced to disputes over ceremonies and even the use of language in the Book of Common Prayer, a related dispute about the relative authority of Scripture, and also to resentment when civil authorities working through bishops and archdeacons attempted to force conformity to Anglican practice. In Scotland, another factor might have been the development of a radical evangelical piety beginning in the 1620s.[49] Some Scottish divines

> began to attack certain customs and liturgical practices of the Kirk which were traditional, but which they claimed were recent innovation—such as saying the Lord's Prayer, singing the doxology at the end of the psalms, and bowing in the pulpit before preaching. There was also a growing preference for extemporaneous prayer.[50]

Scottish Presbyterian worship became more and more austere, bare, and minimalist. Principal Story said that "toward the close of the eighteenth century the public services of the Church of Scotland had become probably the baldest and rudest in Christendom."[51] In such an atmosphere, the liturgical guidelines of the Westminster Directory were probably often ignored, if not actually scorned; and it was during this time that many Presbyterians emigrated to the American colonies. The barrenness of typical Scottish worship, with its indifference even to the simple guidelines of the Directory, became the heritage of American Presbyterians.

In 1788, the American church radically revised the 1644 Directory. The revised American edition of the Directory for Worship, which remained unchanged until past the middle of the twentieth century, institutionalized the minimalism of much Scottish practice.[52] American Directories simply direct that the minister is to "set the elements apart, by prayer and thanksgiving," with no reference at all as to the nature of that thanksgiving. The amended version omits the texts for thanksgiving, Anamnesis, and Epiclesis present in the 1644 version and highlights the Words of Institution, first by directing that they be read immediately after the sermon, either from one of the Gospels or from 1 Corinthians 11. After a description of the exhortation to be made by the minister, the American Directory then includes, as the 1644 version did, a full text of the Words of Institution. Those unfamiliar with the original Directory could be expected to understand the Words of Institution to be of far more importance than the ad hoc thanksgiving, for which no direction is provided. It is not surprising that many American Presbyterians have believed that what really matters in a celebration of the Lord's Supper is that the Words of Institution be said.

The Reformers, contrary to their usual sharp critique of Catholic practice, had followed Roman precedent in the weight they attributed to the Words of Institution. In doing so, they contributed to a sense that the *verba* were, if necessary, sufficient by themselves to make a proper Eucharist, and by precedent they suggested that a prayer of thanksgiving did not require careful attention. American practice hallowed and reinforced this reduced practice. The ultra-Puritan, Pietist, minimally eucharistic sacrament typical of eighteenth-century Scottish and American Presbyterian churches prevailed virtually unchallenged until the second half of the nineteenth century.

4

Reform of Eucharistic
Prayer in Modern Times

Many assume that liturgical recovery in Reformed and other Protestant churches is a relatively recent phenomenon, stimulated perhaps by the Catholic reforms initiated at Vatican Council II. Certainly liturgical reform gained momentum after the council and began to catch the attention of a wider constituency than it had earlier, but critiques of conventional worship in Presbyterian and other churches began to be launched as early as the mid-nineteenth century. A Catholic movement for liturgical reform also has roots in the nineteenth century, although the two movements have no obvious rela tion to one another.[1]

On the European Continent, liturgical developments in Reformed churches had proceeded along different lines than in the English-speaking countries. While the Reformed churches in German-speaking regions tended toward liturgical simplicity to the point of austerity, developments had been different in French-speaking churches. As early as the seventeenth century, not long after the Westminster Assembly, Pastor Jean-Frédéric Ostervald (1663–1747) developed a liturgy for his Swiss congregation in Neuchâtel. The liturgy for the Lord's Supper comes, in large part, from the English Book of Common Prayer. His prayer of "consecration" is taken almost word for word from the BCP.[2]

The Neuchâtel Liturgy of 1713
Trinitarian Invocation
Prayer for Grace
Institution Narrative (1 Corinthians 11)
Exhortation

Reformed Sursum Corda ("Let us lift up our hearts on high . . .")
Proper Prefaces
Pre-Sanctus
Sanctus
Confession
Absolution
Consecration (no Epiclesis, but includes Words of Institution as in BCP)
Distribution[3]

Ostervald encouraged a liturgical sensibility among French-speaking Reformed that continued to distinguish them from German speakers, often aligning them with English-speaking Presbyterians.

One of the most remarkable of the several strands leading to liturgical reform in English-speaking Reformed churches emerged in the mid-nineteenth century, originating in a tiny German Reformed seminary in the obscure village of Mercersburg, Pennsylvania. What has become known as the Mercersburg theology originated as a liturgy presented to the Eastern Synod of the German Reformed Church in 1857. Philip Schaff was its chief architect and the chair of the commission that prepared it, and John Williamson Nevin, formerly a Presbyterian, but more recently a professor in the German Reformed seminary and a member of that denomination, was his colleague and ally.

The *Liturgy, Order of Christian Worship*, which their commission presented to the synod, began the eucharistic portion of the service with the classical opening dialogue including the Sursum Corda ("Lift up your hearts"). The eucharistic prayer included thanksgiving for creation, followed by a section thankfully rehearsing God's work of redemption in Christ, leading to the Sanctus. After the Sanctus come the Words of Institution. The *verba* are not framed as part of the prayer, but rather seem to be an insertion, following the conclusion of one part of the prayer and preceding another. Following the *verba*, the minister says, "Let us pray," leading into an Epiclesis:

> Send down, we beseech Thee, the powerful benediction of Thy Holy Spirit upon these elements of bread and wine, that being set apart now from a common to a sacred and mystical use, they may exhibit the Body and Blood of Thy Son, Jesus Christ; so that in the use of them we may be made, through the power of the Holy Ghost, to partake really and truly of his blessed life.[4]

The Epiclesis concludes with the people's "Amen."

The eucharistic prayer continues at some length with a series of intercessions, each ending with the people's "Amen." The insertion of intercessions here accords with age-old practice in the Eastern churches. The last prayer, one of thanks for "those who have gone before us in the way of salvation," concludes with a petition that we may be joined with them in "the glorious resurrection of the last day." Thanksgiving for the communion of saints, including the departed, also derives from ancient practice. The Lord's Prayer follows, with the minister adding a blessing or benediction upon the congregation in a Trinitarian form. The Mercersburg eucharistic prayer roughly follows the Antiochene model.

SOURCES AND INFLUENCES

The sources of the Mercersburg eucharistic prayer include original contributions of the committee as well as materials drawn from the American Book of Common Prayer, the Palatinate liturgy that was part of the denominational heritage of the German Reformed church, and the liturgy of the Catholic Apostolic Church.[5] Although the Catholic Apostolic Church is not well known today, it played a significant role in the evolution of eucharistic prayer in Reformed churches, in no small part because it provided access to Eastern Orthodox sources. The Catholic Apostolic Church (sometimes called Irvingites) stems from the influence of the Rev. Edward Irving, a minister ordained in the Church of Scotland, although others, particularly John Bate Cardale, had a larger role in the shaping of its polity and worship. The church dates back to an 1832 schism in the Scots church on Regent Square in London. Quite unusually, it combined both charismatic and institutional concerns. Members of the congregation spoke in tongues and harbored apocalyptic expectations, while twelve apostles governed the church, each beginning their apostolate by being assigned to visit twelve regions throughout Europe to do research to guide the new church. By 1835 the church had begun to move to weekly Communion, and it gradually came to focus on the Eucharist as the center of its worship life, drawing from many traditions in the formation of its eucharistic rite. Cardale served as the architect for the church's eucharistic prayer, using a good deal of material from the liturgies of Clement and John Chrysostom, as well as Roman and Anglican sources. It is reminiscent of the Roman Canon in that it is a series of discrete prayers rather than a single, unitary prayer. Cardale's eucharistic theology, interestingly close to that of John Calvin (and the Orthodox), is based on the power of the Holy Spirit.[6]

The Liturgy of the Catholic Apostolic Church
Opening Dialogue
Preface (or Proper Preface)

Sanctus and Benedictus
Lord's Prayer
Epiclesis for the Bread[7]
Words of Institution for the Bread
Epiclesis for the Cup
Words of Institution for the Cup
Oblation
"Special Clause Appointed for the Day or Season"
Anthem at the Time of Offering the Incense
Intercessions, each ending with the people's "Amen"
Commemoration of the Departed
Prayer before Communion (eschatological focus)
    "Christ our Passover is sacrificed for us: therefore let us keep the feast . . ."
Prayer of Humble Access
Agnus Dei
Prayer addressed to "Lord Jesu Christ" [*sic*]
Prayer addressed to "O Holy Ghost"
    "Holy things for holy persons . . ." with response "There is one holy . . ."
Seasonal Benedictions leading to . . .
The Peace
Distribution

The Mercersburg liturgy created a classical eucharistic prayer derived, thanks to the Catholic Apostolic liturgy, from Eastern as well as Western traditions. While not identical to the Antiochene pattern, Mercersburg resembles that form of eucharistic prayer more nearly than it resembles the Roman Canon. The chief difference between the Mercersburg prayer and the Antiochene model is the postponement of the Sanctus to a position after the recital of God's redemptive work in Christ, rather than immediately preceding it, just after the Preface. Clearly, Mercersburg was a departure from Reformed models stemming from Geneva. One student rightly observes that Mercersburg was focused on the theology of the Reformation rather than on its liturgiology. He further comments that "prior to Mercersburg, Reformed theology and Reformed liturgics never came together in any self-conscious, practical way."[8]

The liturgy did not stand alone, unsupported by theological reflection. Nevin was an intense critic of revivalism and the diminished ecclesiology that accompanied it.[9] He wrote extensively about eucharistic theology and its relation to ecclesiology, drawing heavily from a rereading of John Calvin in ways that irked critics formed more by scholastic Calvinism than by Calvin himself—Charles Hodge of Princeton Seminary, in particular.

The tiny Catholic Apostolic Church (Irvingites) influenced not only the Mercersburg liturgy but also developments in nineteenth-century France. Pastor Eugène Bersier (1831–89), a Pietist, was pastor of the Paroisse de l'Étoile in Paris, an evangelical congregation which he led to affiliate with the Reformed Church of France. Bersier believed that the Reformed churches offered the possibility of forming a connection to the common (catholic) tradition, while such a goal was beyond the capability of the evangelical free churches to which he had belonged. Bersier created a liturgy for his own congregation, eventually stirring up a good bit of interest in France and in French-speaking Switzerland in the late nineteenth and early twentieth centuries. The sacraments were important to Bersier, particularly Holy Communion, in which he understood, following in Calvin's footsteps, that Christ "is present and shares himself with those who receive him in faith."[10]

AMERICAN PRESBYTERIAN RENEWAL

In 1864 Charles W. Shields, a professor at Princeton College, published a Presbyterian version of the Book of Common Prayer based on his understanding of the Presbyterian Puritans' petitions at the Savoy Conference of 1661, in which they had sought a revision of the prayer book that would satisfy their objections and achieve reconciliation with the Episcopalians.[11] In Shields's eucharistic service, The Comfortable Words and Prayer of Humble Access precede the opening dialogue.

Presbyterian 1864 Book of Common Prayer
Opening Dialogue
    "It is very meet . . ."
Preface (oriented to thanks and praise, including an Anamnesis)
Sanctus
Epiclesis
Words of Delivery for the Bread, with Breaking of the Bread
Taking of the Cup with Words of Delivery
Distribution
Lord's Prayer

Both the Preface and the Epiclesis include thanksgiving for God's work of redemption in Christ. The Preface does not offer thanks for the creation, nor does it recall God's mighty acts in Israel or the prophets. The Epiclesis is reminiscent of that in Laud's Liturgy, the 1637 Scottish version of the prayer book, but not identical:

> And we most humbly beseech thee, O merciful Father, to hear us; and of thy infinite goodness vouchsafe to bless and sanctify, with thy Word and Holy Spirit, these thy gifts and creatures of bread and wine, that we receiving them, according to our Saviour Christ's institution, in remembrance of his blessed passion and precious death, his mighty resurrection and glorious ascension, and rendering unto thee all possible praise for the same; may by faith be made partakers of his body and blood, with all his benefits, to our spiritual nourishment, and for the glory of thy holy Name.[12]

Once again, Calvinian sensibilities have been addressed in the use of the phrase "thy *Word* and Holy Spirit," as we have seen elsewhere. The prayer has essentially two parts rather than three, the Anamnesis having been folded into the Preface and Epiclesis rather than occupying a place of its own. The Anamnesis is fuller than the English, American, or 1637 Scottish prayer books, with reference not only to Jesus' death, but also to his resurrection and ascension. As in all the versions of the Book of Common Prayer, Shields's version includes an eschatological reference. In this case, it is found in the Preface, "to continue a perpetual memorial of that his precious death, until his coming again." There is no oblation and no thanksgiving for the communion of saints. The Words of Institution, in typical Genevan practice, have been removed from the body of the prayer, and used as a warrant before the exhortation, quoting from 1 Corinthians 11. The Lord's Prayer, rather than immediately following the main body of the eucharistic prayer, follows the Distribution, as in the English and American versions of the BCP.

DEVELOPMENTS IN SCOTLAND

Not long after the appearance in America of the Mercersburg liturgy and Shields's Presbyterian prayer book, similar moves toward some sort of liturgical renewal began to appear in Scotland. Dr. Robert Lee, pastor of Old Greyfriars Kirk in Edinburgh, created a prayer book with an order of service drawn from the 1637 proposed Scottish Book of Common Prayer and from Knox's *Book of Common Order*. Lee's prayer book stirred up resistance and controversy in the Presbytery of Edinburgh, but also had the effect of stimulating a movement for the recovery of the liturgical heritage of the Church of Scotland, represented in particular by the founding of The Church Service Society in 1865.[13]

George Washington Sprott, a minister of the Church of Scotland, had become interested in scholarly research into the liturgical history of the Reformed churches. His discoveries led him first to reprint an edited version of Knox's liturgy, and then, in 1867, to edit a volume published by the Church Service Society called *Euchologion* (also called the *Book of Common Order*).[14] Many subsequent revised editions followed. In the 1905 edition an appendix identifies the several sources for the service of Holy Communion, including Knox's liturgy, Continental Reformed liturgies, and the Book of Common Prayer, but most especially from the Eastern liturgies and those of the (American) German Reformed Church—Mercersburg—and the Catholic Apostolic Church.[15]

Euchologion

Exhortation

Bringing in of the Elements
    "The grace of the Lord Jesus Christ . . ."

Words of Institution

Address

Setting Apart of the Elements

Nicene Creed

Confession and Prayer for Mercy

Agnus Dei

Sursum Corda

Preface "It is very meet . . ." and Anamnesis
    (Christ's incarnation, life, sufferings and death, resurrection, ascension)

Sanctus and Benedictus

Epiclesis

Oblation

Lord's Prayer

Fraction

Distribution of the Bread

Lifting of the Cup

Giving of the Cup

The eucharistic prayer Sprott offered in Euchologion follows the same classic pattern as Mercersburg, distinguishing it from the Roman Canon. Sprott accents the Epiclesis, arguing that

> If the Holy Ghost, by whom the whole body of the Church is governed and sanctified, should be honoured in all acts of worship, this is particularly essential in the Holy Communion. . . . This part of the service is of cardinal importance; and though we may not think the grace and blessing of the Sacrament dependent on our using an

absolutely correct form of words, it is surely blest, as it is easy, to use
a form which unites the suffrages of Christendom, and which no one
can point to as unsatisfactory or insufficient.[16]

While somewhat reminiscent of the Epiclesis described in the 1644 Westminster Directory, Sprott's Epiclesis even more strongly resembles the wording of the 1637 Scottish prayer book.[17] It prays that God may "sanctify with
thy *Word* and Spirit," a coupling of the two that exhibits particular compati-
bility with the Genevan tradition, and is traceable also in various editions of
the Book of Common Prayer, beginning with the 1549 version.

The order for Holy Communion in *Euchologion* was used by the General
Assembly of the Church of Scotland from 1890 to 1923, thus exerting considerable influence on subsequent liturgical forms.[18] The late nineteenth-century
research of Reformed scholars in both Scotland and the United States led to
the production of liturgical materials based on their studies, much of which
contributed to the later publication of officially authorized denominational
materials. For example, in 1923, the Church of Scotland itself published
Prayers for Divine Service, drawn in large part from *Euchologion*.[19]

The Dutch Reformed Church in America published a eucharistic liturgy in
1873 and adopted it officially in 1882. The eucharistic prayer drew, in part,
from the Book of Common Prayer, but far more extensively from *Euchologion*.
The liturgy of the Catholic Apostolic Church also left its mark. A slightly
revised edition became the official liturgy of the denomination in 1906 and
maintained that status until 1968.[20]

THE FIRST *BOOK OF COMMON WORSHIP*

Early in the twentieth century, the General Assembly of the Presbyterian
Church in the United States of America appointed a committee, chaired by
Henry van Dyke, to create a book of forms for worship. Although the resulting book stirred up some controversy, the Assembly nevertheless received it,
and in 1906, the Presbyterian Board of Publication and Sabbath-School Work
published the first *Book of Common Worship* "For Voluntary Use in the
Churches."[21] It includes, of course, a liturgy for Holy Communion, with a
eucharistic prayer. (See Appendix E.)

1906 *Book of Common Worship*
Exhortation
Words of Institution and Setting Apart of the Bread and Cup
Prayer for Forgiveness
Opening Dialogue

Preface "It is very meet . . ." with brief Anamnesis

Sanctus and Benedictus

Oblation

Epiclesis

Trinitarian Doxology with People's "Amen"

Fraction

Distribution of the Bread

Giving of the Cup

The various exhortations typical of Reformed (and Anglican) liturgies, whether from Knox's *Common Order* or editions of the Book of Common Prayer, are all similar. The exhortation in the 1906 *Book of Common Worship* opens with "Dearly beloved, as we draw near to the Lord's Supper to celebrate the Holy Communion of the Body and Blood of Christ," paralleling Knox's liturgy and the BCP.[22] However, the exhortation in the 1906 *BCW* particularly resembles, in part, the contents of the exhortation as prescribed in the 1644 Westminster Directory. Note these parallels:

Westminster	1906 *BCW*
. . . setting forth the great necessity of having	. . . consider earnestly our great need of
our comforts and strength renewed thereby	having our comfort and strength so renewed
in this our pilgrimage and warfare: How	in this our earthly pilgrimage and warfare;
necessary it is that we come unto it with	. . . how necessary it is that we come unto the
Knowledge, Faith, Repentance, Love, and	Lord's Table with knowledge, faith, repentance,
with hungring [*sic*] and thirsting souls after	love, and with hearts hungering and thirsting
Christ and his benefits . . .	after Christ . . .
. . . assuring them, in the same Name, of	Let us therefore so come that we may find
ease, refreshing and strength, to their weak	refreshing and rest unto our souls.
and wearied souls.	

The exhortation comes closer to the BCP when it extends the invitation to the Table to "all that are truly sorry for their sins," similar to "ye who do truly and earnestly repent you of your sins."

After the opening dialogue, the prayer begins with a single Preface focusing on Christ and the Trinity, with no thanksgiving for creation or rehearsing of God's works of redemption in Israel. A brief Anamnesis offers thanks for "the joyful hope of everlasting life through Jesus Christ Thy Son," but no reference is made to his resurrection or ascension. The oblation follows the Sanctus and Benedictus, and, though quite brief, it draws upon language from the BCP. Among several parallels is this, the most striking:

1906 *BCW*	Book of Common Prayer
. . . And here we offer and present, O Lord, ourselves,	And here we offer and present unto thee,
our souls and bodies, to be a reasonable, holy, and	O Lord, our selves, our souls and bodies,
living sacrifice, acceptable unto Thee through Jesus	to be a reasonable, holy, and living
Christ Thy Son.	sacrifice unto thee . . .

The Epiclesis is drawn almost word for word from the 1644 Westminster Directory:

> And we most humbly beseech Thee, Father of all mercies and God of all comfort, to vouchsafe Thy gracious presence, and the effectual working of Thy Spirit in us, and so to sanctify these elements both of Bread and Wine, and to bless Thine own Ordinance; that we may receive by faith Christ crucified for us, and so feed upon Him, that He may be one with us and we with Him; that He may live in us and we in Him who hath loved us, and given Himself for us.

The only eschatological reference in the eucharistic service is in the prayer after Communion, which also contains a memorial of the blessed departed.

In 1929, the Presbyterian Church U.S. (southern) General Assembly approved the republication of the PCUSA's revised edition of the *Book of Common Worship*, which was printed in 1932 as a special edition by the southern church's Commission of Publication in Richmond.[23] The eucharistic prayer in the 1932 edition is almost identical to that in the 1906 book.

CONTINUING RENEWAL EFFORTS IN THE TWENTIETH CENTURY

Challenged by the First World Conference on Faith and Order, held in Lausanne, Switzerland, in 1927, a group of Swiss pastors and interested laypersons organized Church and Liturgy. Its founder, Pastor Richard Paquier (1905–85), had a vision of the church and its worship that might be described as evangelical-catholic. Paquier was well acquainted with liturgical traditions both of the East and of the West and was an enthusiastic admirer of Anglicanism. Church and Liturgy created and distributed "a complete, ecumenically recognizable eucharistic prayer" that appeared in several versions from the 1930s to 1952.[24] It is noteworthy that this group proved to be an inspiration for the liturgical life of the Taizé Community in France, as well as the Grandchamp Community in Switzerland, and inspired the post–World War II liturgy of the French Reformed Church, as well as the *Liturgie à l'usage des Eglises réformées de la Suisse romande* later in the twentieth century.

In 1928 and again in 1940, the Church of Scotland published a *Book of Common Order*.[25] The Service for Holy Communion in the 1940 book begins with the Words of Institution used as a warrant, followed by the opening dialogue, a Preface (with optional Proper Prefaces) followed by the Sanctus and Benedictus, and Anamnesis that refers not only to Christ's suffering and death, but also to his resurrection, ascension, and promise of coming again. The prayer resonates with the cadences and phraseology of the 1637 BCP (Laud's Liturgy). It includes an Epiclesis, which, in a departure from some earlier Reformed liturgies and the American and Scottish versions of the Book of Common Prayer, omits the coupling of "Word and Spirit," that phrase so friendly to Genevan sensibilities. The whole prayer concludes with an ascription of praise to the Holy Trinity, followed by the Great Amen and the Lord's Prayer. The Words of Institution (again) and fraction are followed by the Agnus Dei, words of delivery, Distribution, and the Peace (verbal only).

The PCUSA General Assembly authorized a revision of the *Book of Common Worship*, which was published in 1946.[26]

1946 *Book of Common Worship*

Invitation to the Table

Words of Institution

Opening Dialogue

Preface "It is very meet . . ." (provision for Proper Prefaces)

Sanctus (no Benedictus)

Anamnesis (incarnation and holy life, passion, death and resurrection, ascension, continual intercession)

Epiclesis

Oblation

Trinitarian Doxology

Lord's Prayer

Fraction
Lifting of the Cup
Agnus Dei
Distribution

While the Epiclesis is reminiscent of the 1906 *BCW* and the 1644 Westminster Directory, it diverges considerably from those texts. Following the example of the 1940 Scottish *BCO*, it prays God "to bless and sanctify with Thy Holy Spirit both us and these Thy gifts of bread and wine," leaving out any reference to the Word, and thus distinguishing itself from American and Scottish versions of the BCP. In this omission as well as in the rest of the Epiclesis, the 1946 *BCW* follows nearly word for word the Epiclesis in the 1940 Scottish *Book of Common Order*. The Anamnesis in the 1946 American *BCW* also follows closely that in the 1940 Scottish book, while the oblation is nearly identical with that in both the 1906 *BCW* and the 1940 Scottish *BCO*.

5

A Crescendo of Consensus

At the midpoint of the twentieth century, a remarkable consensus had already arisen among the historic churches and was gathering momentum. After World War II, the German Protestant Michael Brotherhood (*Michaelsbrüder-schaft*) established a branch in German-speaking Switzerland that included a small, but influential, group of Reformed ministers and laity. They accented the sacramental life of the church, promoting more frequent celebration of the Eucharist and the development of a fuller eucharistic liturgy, in particular, eucharistic prayer.[1]

While Karl Barth, another German-Swiss, did not display interest in liturgical forms, his theology nevertheless influenced the development of eucharistic prayer in German-speaking churches. In a little book on preaching, Barth had declared that "there is indeed no preaching, in the precise meaning of the term, except when it is accompanied and illuminated by the sacrament."[2] Some who had been profoundly impressed by Karl Barth's thought created the *Baselbieter Kirchenbuch* (Liturgy of Basel-Campagne) in 1949. While simple in the best Reformed sense of that word, it nevertheless "gracefully and without making a point of it, brings the elements of eucharistic celebration from the common church tradition into the Reformed liturgy."[3]

Meanwhile, in the United States, the PCUS (southern Presbyterian church) in 1963 published, as part of its *Book of Church Order*, the Directory for the Worship and Work of the Church. The 1788 American revision of the Directory for Worship had remained unchanged (except for minor revisions in the so-called "southern" church's Directory) until twentieth-century revisions. The tone of the DWW tended toward the somber and the penitential, and its theology tilts sometimes toward Zwingli and sometimes toward Calvin. However, guidelines for the eucharistic prayer include not only those forms that are indigenous to the Reformed tradition, such as the use of the Words of Institution as a warrant; interpretation of the theological significance of the sacrament as part of the liturgy; an invitation; and fencing/exhortation. They also call for a prayer of thanksgiving "which shall include remembrance of the death and resurrection of Christ, and shall ask that the Holy Spirit sanctify the Sacrament unto the people's benefit."[4] In other words, the DWW calls for eucharistic prayer that includes thanksgiving, Anamnesis, and Epiclesis.

The United Presbyterian Church in the U.S.A. (a union of the former Presbyterian Church in the United States of America and the United Presbyterian Church in North America) revised its Directory in 1961, harvesting the fruits of twentieth-century liturgical research. The revised Directory focuses on the Eucharist as a celebration of Christ's resurrection rather than simply a commemoration of his death. The eucharistic prayer as described in the 1961 Directory begins with the use of the Words of Institution as a warrant; then requires a prayer of thanksgiving including an Anamnesis ("a solemn and joyous remembrance of Christ") and an Epiclesis. The Directory says that "The invocation of the Holy Spirit signifies and seeks to ensure that what takes place in the sacrament is not accomplished by human endeavor, but is done by the grace of God."[5]

In 1962, the Synod of the Church of South India (CSI) approved its own liturgy in a volume called *The Book of Common Worship*. The Church of South India was created by the union of former Anglican, Presbyterian, Congregational, and Methodist churches, and the publication of its liturgy was a significant ecumenical milestone. The eastern Liturgy of Saint James (end of the fourth or early fifth century) served as the CSI's primary source for recovering the classical heritage of eucharistic prayer.[6] Since a version of Saint James is still in use in the Mar Thoma Syrian Church in India (a church with particular strength in south India), the influence of the ancient liturgy upon the newer eucharistic prayer of the Church of South India should not be surprising. Following the Antiochene form, the CSI eucharistic prayer set the pattern for many others published subsequently in the service books of a number of denominations.

THE MODEL OF THE CHURCH OF SOUTH INDIA

The Church of South India anaphora begins with the traditional opening dialogue, followed by a Preface that recalls God's creation of the heavens and the earth and speaks of God's having redeemed a sinful humanity "to be the first-fruits of a new creation."[7] The book offers Proper Prefaces appropriate to the season. The Sanctus and Benedictus follow, leading into a Post-Sanctus very reminiscent of the Book of Common Prayer, including the Words of Institution within the body of the prayer.

For the first time in a Protestant liturgy, we find a Memorial Acclamation, even before the Second Vatican Council's updated version of the Roman Canon. As in the Roman Canon, the acclamation follows the *verba* relating to the cup. It comes from the (Syriac) Anaphora of the Twelve Apostles, dating to about AD 400: "Amen. Thy death, O Lord, we commemorate, thy resurrection we confess, and thy second coming we await. Glory be to thee, O Christ."[8] Rather than ending with the *verba* and Memorial Acclamation, the Post-Sanctus continues. The continuing Anamnesis is reminiscent of both the Scottish and American Book of Common Prayer and of the 1940 Scottish *Book of Common Order*, recalling Christ's death and passion, resurrection and ascension, and anticipating his coming again, followed once more by an acclamation by the congregation: "We give thanks to thee, we praise thee, we glorify thee, O Lord our God." The acclamation is almost identical to that found in the Eastern liturgies of St. John Chrysostom and St. Basil the Great.[9]

The Epiclesis resembles that in the 1940 Scottish *BCO*, a liturgy also believed to have been influenced by the Anaphora of Saint James: "And we most humbly beseech thee, O merciful Father, to sanctify with thy Holy Spirit us and these thine own gifts of bread and wine . . ."[10] The eucharistic prayer ends with an ascription of praise to the Holy Trinity and the people's Amen.

In 1970 the UPCUSA published *The Worshipbook: Services*.[11] Called "The Thanksgiving," the eucharistic prayer begins with the opening dialogue followed by a Preface offering thanks to God for creating the world, "commandments to Moses" and "the cry of the prophets." Proper Prefaces are also provided. Then follow the Sanctus (two options, one including the Benedictus); and an Anamnesis that recalls Christ's ministry ("He told your story, healed the sick, and was a friend of sinners"), his death and resurrection, and the promise of the kingdom. For the first time in an American Protestant service book, there is a version of the Memorial Acclamation: "Remembering the Lord Jesus, we break bread and share one cup, announcing his death for the sins of the world, and telling his resurrection to all men and nations."[12]

The Epiclesis leads to an oblation, spoken by the congregation, and the Lord's Prayer. There is no Trinitarian doxology, no indication that intercessions might be included after the Epiclesis, and no memorial of the faithful departed. The Words of Institution are used after the prayer, accompanying the fraction and libation. The entire prayer is brief and compact.

The 1979 Scottish *Book of Common Order* follows the same (Antiochene) model of eucharistic prayer as its 1940 predecessor, though in a somewhat expanded version; however, in a departure from most Reformed precedents, it includes the Words of Institution within the prayer. This sparked a good deal of controversy, and the publisher subsequently included a printed slip to be included in every volume, to the effect that, in the Scottish tradition, the Words of Institution are recited as a warrant. Following Mercersburg (as well as ancient Eastern patterns), the 1979 *BCO* makes a place after the Epiclesis for the inclusion of intercessions.[13] It concludes with a memorial of the blessed departed and the Lord's Prayer.

The Scottish *Book of Common Order* of 1994 continues in the precedents established in the earlier books, with the exception of revisiting the question of the placement of the Words of Institution. In the 1994 book, the institution narrative normally precedes the opening dialogue, although provision is made for exceptions.[14] An interesting feature of the 1994 eucharistic service is that a rubric names that portion of the service in which "the offerings of money, along with the gifts of bread and wine, are brought to the Communion Table" as "The Great Entrance," following the nomenclature of the Eastern churches.[15] While the practice of presenting the bread and wine at the table at the offertory is traditional in the Church of Scotland, the explicit link with the practice of the Orthodox churches is new.

The United Reformed Church (URC) in England and Wales is a union of the Presbyterian and Congregational churches, joined later by some congregations of the Churches of Christ (Disciples). The URC liturgy, published in 1980, includes a description of the basic elements and order of the eucharistic prayer, following the Antiochene form that has become the ecumenical norm.[16]

The United Reformed Eucharistic Prayer

Invitation

The Peace

Offertory, including Presentation of the Bread and Wine

Offertory Prayer

Narrative of the Institution

Opening Dialogue

Preface (or Proper Preface)

Sanctus and Benedictus

Anamnesis

Epiclesis

Oblation

Trinitarian Doxology

Great Amen

The Lord's Prayer
Distribution

A second order includes a Memorial Acclamation.

The German-speaking Reformed churches of Switzerland published their *Liturgie* in 1983.[17] It shows the profound influence of ecumenical norms, all the more remarkable considering that German-speaking Reformed churches have more typically followed a tradition of liturgical minimalism. Curiously, the First Order introduces the Epiclesis *before* the Words of Institution, following contemporary Roman practice rather than Antiochene. In this order, but not in all, the Words of Institution are included within the eucharistic prayer rather than used either as a warrant immediately preceding it, or after it just before the distribution, either of these practices being more typical among Reformed churches. In the Second Order, in which the institution narrative is also included within the prayer rather than outside it, the Epiclesis *follows* the *verba*.

Swiss German–First Order

Invitation
Offertory, including Presentation of Bread and Wine
Offertory Prayer
Opening Dialogue
Proper Preface
Sanctus and Benedictus
Epiclesis
Words of Institution
Memorial Acclamation
Anamnesis
Trinitarian Doxology and Amen (whole congregation)
Lord's Prayer
The Peace
Agnus Dei
Distribution

The Second Order makes use of the traditional Orthodox "Holy things for holy people!" followed by the classic response, "One is holy, our Lord Jesus Christ." The Third Order is Zwingli's, the Fourth is Oecolampadius's, and the Fifth is Calvin's. There are fourteen orders, followed by three for a "small group" (kleinen Kreis); one for home Communion or Communion with the sick; another for the very ill and one with the dying. The book includes a number of options that may be substituted for various elements of the fully printed orders. An auxiliary volume provides musical settings for the Eucharist, including a Sanctus, Memorial Acclamation, Agnus Dei, and Amen.[18]

LATE TWENTIETH-CENTURY SERVICE BOOKS

The emergence of something resembling ecumenical consensus is best expressed by the World Council of Churches' document *Baptism, Eucharist and Ministry*, published in 1982. Produced by the WCC's Faith and Order Commission, *BEM* is truly ecumenical. The Faith and Order Commission included not only members from virtually all the confessional traditions, but also among its full members theologians of the Roman Catholic Church and churches of other traditions that do not belong to the WCC.[19]

BEM defines the Eucharist as "essentially the sacrament of the gift which God makes to us in Christ through the power of the Holy Spirit."[20] The same document describes the Eucharist in Trinitarian terms:

> thanksgiving to the Father
> memorial of Christ
> invocation of the Spirit[21]

The commentary in *BEM* discusses the traditional ecumenical debate about whether the Words of Institution, or perhaps the Epiclesis, actually effect the sacrament. The commentary expresses the hope that the churches might move beyond this impasse, recovering the viewpoint most common in early centuries, that the entire prayer action effected the Eucharist, rather than simply one part of it.[22]

Exhibiting the growing consensus expressed in *BEM*, the 1986 Swiss French Liturgy makes use of four eucharistic prayers.[23] Two are original, and two are revisions of the prayer in *Apostolic Tradition* (AD 215). They are quite similar to the Great Thanksgivings in the 1993 Presbyterian *Book of Common Worship*. They include Words of Institution, an Anamnesis with oblations, and an Epiclesis.

In the same year, 1986, the United Church of Christ published *Book of Worship: United Church of Christ*.[24] Its eucharistic prayers roughly conform to the familiar ecumenical pattern.

United Church of Christ *Book of Worship*–Option A
Invitation
Opening Dialogue

Preface and Anamnesis
Sanctus and Benedictus
Words of Institution
Memorial Acclamation
Epiclesis
Oblation (in Option B)
Intercessions may be inserted here
Lord's Prayer
Fraction and Libation
Agnus Dei
Distribution

The Anamnesis (or Post-Sanctus), recalling God's redemptive work in Christ, is included in the Preface rather than following the Sanctus, thus obscuring the tripartite or Trinitarian form of the prayer. The prayer includes a Trinitarian doxology to precede the Lord's Prayer, although it is not clear whether the "Amen" is intended to be said by the people. The *Book of Worship* provides a section of musical settings for use in the eucharistic prayer, but there is none for the Great Amen. In the interests of avoiding gender-exclusive language, the word "Lord" does not appear. The opening dialogue is framed

God be with you.
And also with you.
Lift up your hearts.
We lift them up to God.
Let us give thanks to God Most High.
It is right to give God thanks and praise.

Similarly the Lord's Prayer is called Prayer of Our Savior. In the UCC second order, the Lord's Prayer is denoted as such but prayed before the opening of the eucharistic service. In both orders, the Words of Institution are included within the prayer, following ecumenical custom, with no option for use outside the prayer, as has been more common in the Reformed tradition.

PRESBYTERIAN DEVELOPMENTS

After the 1983 reunion of the separated (so-called southern and northern) denominations (PCUS and UPCUSA), the newly formed American church adopted in 1989 a new Directory for Worship that reflects the ecumenical consensus. The Directory sets forth a specific form to be followed when offering the Great Thanksgiving, including thanksgiving for creation and providence, for covenant history, and for seasonal blessings, with an acclamation of praise (presumably, Sanctus and Benedictus); an Anamnesis in which the church remembers God's acts of salvation in Jesus Christ, mentioning his birth, life, death, resurrection, and promise of coming again, and his institution of the Supper "if not otherwise spoken," together with an acclamation of faith (a Memorial Acclamation); an Epiclesis, calling upon the Holy Spirit to draw the people into the presence of the risen Christ; followed by an ascription of praise to the Triune God and the Lord's Prayer.[25]

The 1993 PCUSA *Book of Common Worship* (which is also the official service book of the Cumberland Presbyterian Church), is consistent with the 1989 Directory. It contains twenty-four eucharistic prayers, called Great Thanksgivings, for use in the Service for the Lord's Day. The "default setting," Great Thanksgiving A (p. 69 ff.) in the Service for the Lord's Day, is typical.[26] (See chapter 6 for a fuller treatment of Great Thanksgiving A, and see Appendix H for the text.)

Great Thanksgiving A, PCUSA 1993 *BCW*

Opening Dialogue

Preface

Sanctus and Benedictus

Post-Sanctus (Anamnesis)

(Words of Institution included here, or outside the prayer)

Oblation

Memorial Acclamation

Epiclesis

Intercessions

Thanksgiving for "all your saints"

Ascription of Praise to the Holy Trinity

Great Amen

Lord's Prayer

Fraction and Lifting of the Cup

Distribution

There is no Agnus Dei, in the interests of downplaying the all-too-frequent penitential cast of the Eucharist, although provision is made for its use as one of several possible sung responses after the Prayer of Confession.[27]

A supplemental book of service music called *Holy Is the Lord: Music for Lord's Day Worship*, published in 2003 by the PCUSA, offers musical texts for the Service for the Lord's Day.[28] It includes congregational acclamations and responses for use in celebrating the sacraments of Baptism and the Eucharist, including multiple settings of the Sanctus and Benedictus, Memorial Acclamations, and the Great Amen. The musical styles are diverse, including African-American and Hispanic as well as classical and contemporary settings. Some settings, including that of Presbyterian composer Hal Hopson, offer music to be used by the presider in singing parts of the eucharistic prayer, for example, the opening dialogue, the Pre-Sanctus ("Therefore we praise you . . ."), the introduction to the Memorial Acclamation ("Great is the mystery of faith."), and the Trinitarian Doxology before the Great Amen.

ENGLAND AND FRANCE

The new (2000) Anglican prayer book, *Common Worship: Services and Prayers for the Church of England*,[29] is meant to supplement the 1662 Book of Common Prayer, although it is as complete a book as the traditional BCP. It includes services for Holy Communion designated Order One and Order Two. Order One offers eight eucharistic prayers, A through H. Order Two is the authorized 1662 order, first in traditional English, then in contemporary language. In contrast to the older English BCP, the prayers in Order One include an Epiclesis. Similar to the alternative Roman Catholic eucharistic prayers, Prayers A and B use a double Epiclesis, one before the Words of Institution, over the gifts of bread and wine, and one after the Memorial Acclamation, over the people.[30] Prayers C and E make use of a single Epiclesis immediately preceding the Words of Institution.[31] The Epiclesis of Prayer C seems to be a prayer for the Spirit's work in the people, without directly praying that the Spirit bless or sanctify the gifts of bread and wine. Prayers D, F, G, and H contain a single Epiclesis, in the Antiochene pattern, after the Words of Institution: "Send your Spirit on us now that by these gifts we may feed on Christ."[32] Several of these prayers invite congregational acclamations periodically throughout the prayer. Prayers A and C are also available "in Traditional Language."

The Reformed Church of France introduced a new liturgy in 1996.[33] It offers several options for the eucharistic service. None begins with the traditional opening dialogue. Ordinarily, the first part of the service is the Preface, understood as a confession of faith, and most often structured in a Trinitarian form.

Preface–Culte Dominicale 1
It is our joy to glorify you, O God our Father,
for this world that you have created so fair
and that you guard in the midst of its sorrows
until the day when, according to your promise,
your kingdom shall come.

It is our joy to glorify you for your Son,
Jesus Christ, our Lord, born of our flesh, baptized,
tempted, transfigured, condemned, crucified,
resurrected from among the dead, raised in glory.

It is our joy to glorify you for your breath of life,
the Spirit of adoption who teaches us to call you Father,
who drives out our fears and kindles our faith.

So, with the heavens and the earth,
with the multitude of your people,
of all times and all places,
we glorify your name [and sing]. (author's translation)

A sung response (Chant spontané) follows, in the position of the Sanctus and Benedictus. Most often, the Words of Institution come next, preceding the Communion Prayer (Prière de Communion), which is both an Anamnesis (a memorial of Christ's death and resurrection and anticipation of his coming again) and an Epiclesis. In some of the forms, the memorial of Jesus includes reference to his incarnation, baptism, temptation, transfiguration, condemnation, crucifixion, resurrection, and ascension. The prayers are sensitive to the eschatological dimension of the meal. In some instances, the intercessions are included in the prayer, following the Epiclesis. The Lord's Prayer is always used. Each of the forms includes actions described as Fraction et Elevation, the breaking of the bread and the lifting of the cup, sometimes just before the Distribution, or between the Sanctus and the combined Anamnesis/Epiclesis (Prière de Communion); sometimes in relation to the Words of Institution and sometimes not. The Introduction to the *Liturgie* describes the Fraction and Elevation as "the essential element of this ritual rooted in the Jewish tradition."[34] The English Puritans assembled for the Savoy Conference held similar views. There is in the French liturgy no use of a Memorial Acclamation or Great Amen. The breaking of the eucharistic action into discrete parts under distinct headings gives the appearance of a series of prayers linked together after the fashion of the Roman Canon, even though it is possible to discern the Antiochene form in this compactly worded anaphora.

THE NETHERLANDS AND GERMANY

In the Netherlands, three churches joined together in 1998 to publish a service book: the Netherlands Reformed Church, the Christian Reformed Churches in the Netherlands (Gereformeerde), and the Evangelical-Lutheran Church in the Netherlands.[35] There are forty-two eucharistic prayers! Gen-

erally, they follow the Antiochene pattern, with a Preface, Sanctus and Benedictus, Post-Sanctus, institution narrative, a Memorial Acclamation, an Epiclesis, the Great Amen, and Lord's Prayer. Option A follows the Lord's Prayer
with the Peace, leading to the Agnus Dei. In Option B, rubrics specifically call
for the breaking of the bread and the lifting of the cup. Musical texts are provided for the congregation's participation in the dialogues and acclamations of
the prayer. While it is difficult to generalize about such a large number of
prayers, Prefaces are likely to give thanks for the created world. The Words
of Institution are included within the prayer. There is always an Epiclesis, and
the prayers may recall the faithful departed, with all the saints. The prayers
recognize the eschatological dimensions of the meal. This multioptions book
also includes both the traditional Dutch Reformed liturgy established in Dor-
drecht in 1578 and Calvin's liturgy.

The Reformed Federation of Germany published a liturgy in 1999.[36] It
includes four eucharistic settings, ranging from very simple to fuller. Among
the four options, the Words of Institution may be included either before the
eucharistic prayer or within the body of the prayer, in the Post-Sanctus. The
eucharistic prayers themselves tend to be brief but may include thanksgiving
for creation and always include some form of Anamnesis and an Epiclesis. Two
of the forms offer the option of Proper Prefaces. Form B1 includes the classic
opening dialogue, Sanctus and Benedictus, and Memorial Acclamation. Form
B2 includes the opening dialogue and Sanctus and Benedictus. B1 follows the
order Lord's Prayer, the Peace, Agnus Dei, while B2 follows the order Lord's
Prayer, Words of Institution, Agnus Dei. Two of the forms provide rubrics
calling for the breaking of the bread and the giving of the cup. None invites
the congregation to offer the Great Amen.

THE UNITED CHURCH OF CANADA

Celebrate God's Presence, the *Book of Services* of the United Church of Canada,
an early-twentieth-century union of three churches (Congregational,
Methodist, and Presbyterian) includes eleven eucharistic prayers, the first of
which (Prayer A) is an outline for the presider to use in extemporaneous prayer
or as a guide to creating an original prayer.[37] The descriptions of the prayer in
the *Book of Services* use contemporary designations, but the list of elements
here is given in traditional terminology.

Celebrate God's Presence–United Church of Canada
Opening Dialogue or Sursum Corda
Preface

Sanctus and Benedictus
Post-Sanctus
Words of Institution
Anamnesis–Oblation
Memorial Acclamation
Epiclesis
Trinitarian Doxology
Great Amen
Lord's Prayer

Like the United Church of Christ, the United Church of Canada has altered some of the traditional liturgical language for the sake of inclusiveness. For example, the opening dialogue proceeds as follows:

May God be with us.
God is here among us.
Let us open our hearts to God.
We open them to God and to one another.
Let us give thanks to God.
It is right to give our thanks and praise.

United Church of Canada Prayer B includes the possibility of questions from a child (similar to the Jewish Passover haggadah) asked and answered within the context of the prayer, for example, "Why do we eat bread at this table?" Answer: "We gather at this table to remember that on the night before he died . . ."[38] Intercessions may be included before, rather than after, the Epiclesis. The prayer ends with a Trinitarian doxology and the Great Amen. Musical settings are published in another volume. Prayer C uses traditional "Lord" language, both in English and in a French version of the prayer. When it names the members of the Trinity, however, it employs the familiar compromise, "Creator, Christ, and Spirit." The Lord's Prayer is named "The Prayer of Jesus."

Prayer F is composed in a poetic style, with congregational acclamations prompted by the presider. The Epiclesis proceeds as follows:

Holy God, we beg for your Spirit.
Enliven this bread,
Awaken this body,
Pour us out for each other.
Transfigure our minds,
Ignite your church,
Nourish the life of the earth.
Make us, while many, united,

Make us, though broken, whole,
Make us, despite death, alive.

And so we cry, Come, Holy Spirit:
   Come, Holy Spirit!
And so the church shouts, Come, Holy Spirit:
   Come, Holy Spirit!
And so the earth pleads, Come, Holy Spirit:
   Come, Holy Spirit!

The Trinitarian Doxology is in the style of a Celtic prayer:

You, Holy God, Holy One, Holy Three,
Our Life, our Mercy, our Might,
Our Table, our Food, our Server,
Our Rainbow, our Ark, our Dove,
Our Sovereign, our Water, our Wine,
Our Light, our Treasure, our Tree,
Our Way, our Truth, our Life.
You, Holy God, Holy One, Holy Three!
Praise now,
Praise tomorrow,
Praise forever.

Prayer I is the ancient prayer of Hippolytus of Rome (ca. 215), which is becoming familiar from its inclusion in a variety of contemporary service books. Prayer J, described as "particularly suitable for use when Communion is celebrated in the home or hospital," is a brief prayer, including no congregational acclamations except for the Great Amen. Prayer K, even briefer, nevertheless intentionally includes traditional eucharistic themes: "praise, thanksgiving, remembrance, offering, invocation of the Spirit, and longing for God's reign."[39] (See Appendix G.) Both Prayer J and Prayer K presume that the Words of Institution will be used outside the body of the prayer.

ECUMENICAL AND AMERICAN REFORMED

The vast majority of the world's Christians belong to churches that at least commend the praying of the Eucharist in this emerging ecumenical, Trinitarian pattern. Of course, in the Orthodox churches, the anaphora of *The Divine Liturgy of Saint John Chrysostom*, as well as that of the liturgy of St. Basil, represents this tradition, and the new Roman prayers follow it as well, with the exception that the Roman prayers introduce an Epiclesis before the *verba*.

As for Reformed churches, the Presbyterian service books published in

Ireland, Wales, and New Zealand, like the examples cited above, also represent the ecumenical consensus, having been shaped largely by the Antiochene
model. The emerging ecumenical consensus is equally represented in the late-
twentieth-century and early-twenty-first-century service books of other
denominations, such as *The United Methodist Book of Worship*,[40] the *Lutheran
Book of Worship*,[41] and the American Episcopal *The Book of Common Prayer*.[42]
The latter book offers an interesting contrast in that Holy Eucharist: Rite
One, maintaining the liturgy of the 1928 prayer book, includes in the Epicle-
sis the link between "Word" and "Spirit": "vouchsafe to bless and sanctify, with
thy Word and Holy Spirit, these thy gifts and creatures of bread and wine."[43]
This is, of course, the language of Cranmer's 1549 prayer book and the 1637
Scottish book as well. The newer liturgy, represented in Holy Eucharist: Rite
Two, omits "Word," and reads, "Sanctify them [these gifts] by your Holy
Spirit."[44]

The eucharistic liturgy of the Reformed Church in America takes the
Antiochene form. The Post-Sanctus, commemorating God's work in
Christ, is quite brief but lifts up Christ's death, resurrection, and promise
of coming again, and concludes with an oblation. There is a full Epiclesis,
but there is no Trinitarian doxology and no indication of a Great Amen. At
its conclusion, the prayer borrows the evocative words of the second-
century *Didache*:

> And as this grain has been gathered from many fields into one loaf,
> and these grapes from many hills into one cup, grant, O Lord, that
> your whole Church may soon be gathered from the ends of the earth
> into your kingdom. Even so, come, Lord Jesus![45]

The Words of Institution follow the prayer.

The Christian Reformed Synod in 1994 approved a form for the Eucharist
that serves as a revision of their 1981 Service of Word and Sacrament, in which
the eucharistic service followed the classic Antiochene form.[46] Introductory
notes in 1994 say that "in setting forth the meaning of this sacrament, the
Reformed confessions, the writings of Reformed theologians, and recent ecumenical documents emphasize the following themes:

> The Lord's Supper is a thanksgiving to God. (Eucharist)
> The Lord's Supper is a memorial of Christ. (Anamnesis)
> The Lord's Supper is a participation in the body and the blood of Christ.
> The Lord's Supper signifies the work of the Spirit. (Epiclesis)
> The Lord's Supper symbolizes the unity of the church in all times and places.
> The Lord's Supper seals the present and coming kingdom of God."[47]

Similarly, the Synod describes four actions:

> taking bread and wine
> giving thanks over them
> breaking the bread/pouring the wine
> sharing among God's people

> **1994 Christian Reformed Option One**
> Offertory (suggests bringing bread and wine to the table at this point)
> Opening Dialogue
> Preface (or Proper Preface)
> Sanctus
> Words of Institution
> Memorial Acclamation
> Epiclesis
> Lord's Prayer
> Invitation
> Distribution

The Words of Institution are used within the prayer, as part of it, followed immediately by a Memorial Acclamation. There is no Post-Sanctus (Anamnesis), although the Prefaces typically make mention, very briefly, of christological themes.

The CRC 1994 liturgy also offers three alternative eucharistic services, the second employing congregational song in place of the Preface.[48] The Sanctus is sung after the Epiclesis, and followed by a Memorial Acclamation. Setting three is a variation on the second, making use of extensive biblical quotations and also employing congregational hymnody as part of the prayer. It is not clear whether there is an Epiclesis, although the form calls for a "Prayer of Consecration," which might suppose an invocation of the Holy Spirit. The fourth setting is an adaptation of confessional documents and Reformation writings. Words of Institution are used at the beginning as a warrant. The "Prayer of Consecration" is meant to be offered by all in unison. There is no true Epiclesis. None of the settings makes use of a concluding Trinitarian doxology or Great Amen.

REFORMED EUCHARISTIC PRAYER IN TRINITARIAN PERSPECTIVE

Commenting on the fruits of a Reformed consultation on worship in Geneva in 1994, Bruno Bürki comments that in the newer liturgies, the Eucharist is placed in a trinitarian perspective. This approach is remarkable in the Reformed tradition, which has hitherto been set in a christological pattern. . . . The Reformed churches have rediscovered the great Eucharistic prayer of thanksgiving as a trinitarian confession . . . and it contributes to the liturgy—like theology—becoming doxology.[49]

Bürki comments further that the full development of the Trinitarian dimensions of the Eucharist prevents disastrous fragmentation, such as

- the splitting apart of crucifixion and resurrection (making the Eucharist a sacrament of the cross alone)
- the splitting apart of past and present (making the Lord's Supper into a historical observance)
- the splitting apart of atonement and sanctification (making the Eucharist into a penitential rite)
- a splitting apart of Christ and the Holy Spirit (making the Lord's Supper vulnerable to ideology and incapable of shaping spirituality).[50]

OFFICIAL TEXTS VERSUS ACTUAL PRACTICE

The various examples cited in this book do not exhaust the possibilities. Reformed churches exist in at least 180 countries, and in many cases, more than one Reformed church exists in the same country. Reformed Christians prepare their official documents in many languages, including many non-European languages. The examples in this book come, for the most part, from churches in Europe and North America. Whatever service books may have been published in Asia, Africa, or Latin America have not been included in this study (although, there is a Korean version of the PCUSA's *Book of Common Worship*).[51] For this reason, at least, it is not possible to make sweeping or conclusive statements about the extent to which Reformed churches throughout the world, particularly in the southern hemisphere, have come to advocate the use of classical and ecumenical forms of eucharistic prayer.

In particular, since Reformed churches have typically presumed a good deal of freedom in practice, even when there are liturgical guidelines in place, it is not possible to know whether ministers and congregations are actually using official texts of eucharistic prayers, either as published, or as models for locally drafted prayers. Even taking American Presbyterians alone, it is only a matter of speculation how many congregations actually make use of the forms of prayer published in the various editions of the *Book of Common Worship*.

Taking an optimistic point of view, it would seem probable that the 1993 *BCW* is exerting more and more influence on public worship in ecclesiastical governing bodies and, by their example, becoming known and used in local congregations. After all, before the 1906 *Book of Common Worship*, few congregations made use of a communal prayer of confession, but in the years and decades following its publication, the practice became almost ubiquitous. One might imagine that the 1993 *BCW* will have similar influence over time. However, with the growth in the number of so-called "contemporary" services, it is not possible to take such an influence for granted.

Earlier editions of the *BCW* have provided a number of models of eucharistic prayer that are attentive to the traditional contents of classical prayer and to the form and structure of classical eucharistic prayer as well. Even so, it is common to find a Presbyterian service in which the Words of Institution are prominent but eucharistic prayer is almost nonexistent. One may hear the equivalent of a brief table grace, with no Trinitarian form, no rehearsal of God's mighty acts in creation or in Christ, and, most astonishingly in a Reformed setting, no prayer for the Holy Spirit to bless us and the gifts of bread and wine. Sometimes one may hear what begins as a classical eucharistic prayer but concludes prematurely, with no Anamnesis, no Epiclesis, and no Trinitarian doxology, much like Luther's eucharistic prayer, which ends abruptly after the Words of Institution. The Great Amen is almost universally unsaid and unsung, and frequently there is no indication by the presider that it is known or expected.

What is true of Presbyterian churches is, I am certain, true also in the United Church of Christ, the United Church of Canada, the Reformed and Christian Reformed churches, and quite likely in European Reformed churches and their offspring in other parts of the world. As churches, the minimalism of the Directory tradition and the cherished freedom of liturgical practice have created a situation in which the study of the history, theology, and practice of Christian worship has claimed only small attention in our seminaries, some of which require no course in worship at all. Only in the last decade or so, under the pressure of the baby-boom generation and the movement toward "contemporary" and "seeker" worship, have ministers and lay members exhibited strong interest in worship issues, leaving the Great Tradition of the church almost wholly disarmed and undefended in a tidal wave of worship experiments based more on pragmatic assessments and panic about numbers than on careful, reflective, and knowledgeable consideration.

THE TRADITION OF CALVIN

Does it matter what we do liturgically, as long as we have our confessional documents in the right order? Calvin's eucharistic theology was better than his liturgy. His liturgy embodies theological insights that were important to him and to the church in the midst of the Reformation conflicts, but under the pressure exerted by the crisis, some things have been exaggerated and other things neglected. The concern for understanding the liturgy leads to an oppressive didacticism that often persists even today, while Calvin's theology of the Holy Spirit seems hardly to have made an impression on his eucharistic liturgy. In the Reformed tradition, theology and liturgical practice seem capable of being walled off from each other, so that a sophisticated theological understanding of the sacraments, for example, doesn't always require an equally subtle attention to its liturgical expression. It is as though the transmission of a theological vision functions independently, perhaps by classroom study or ecclesiastical action, while Lord's Day worship may or may not represent that vision adequately.

The history of service books in Reformed churches over the past one hundred years sees a consistent move toward a fuller eucharistic liturgy. While service books may include eucharistic prayers and/or forms rooted in the sixteenth-century Reformation, those are almost never the first options. The first options, in many cases the only options, are more likely to be informed by a deeper, longer, and more ecumenical tradition, including that of the Eastern church. The *ordo* of these eucharistic prayers is not always the same. Even classical elements of eucharistic prayer may be ordered differently so as to accent one theological insight rather than another. In nearly every case, however, Reformed eucharistic prayers since as early as the seventeenth century make use of an explicit Epiclesis, rooted in Calvin's eucharistic theology, but also, of course, in Eastern theology and practice. The Epiclesis would seem to be, for Reformed people, the sine qua non of a liturgy informed by Calvin's thought. Insofar as the Reformed tradition has anything to say to the whole church about Eucharist, it would seem that we need to say Amen to Calvin's affirmation of a theology informed by sources Eastern as well as Western, that is, to his eucharistic theology rooted in the action of the Holy Spirit.

6

Eucharistic Prayer
Ecumenical and Reformed

Even a cursory review of the minutes of the seventeenth-century Westminster Assembly's debates over the first Directory for Worship reveals that the members of the assembly strongly believed that every word and action of the liturgy made a theological statement, and that it mattered what those theological statements might be. That perspective squares very well with the traditional saying "Lex orandi, lex credendi," meaning, very broadly, that the way we pray shapes the way we believe. From a twenty-first century point of view, the Puritans gathered at Westminster took a rather narrow view of what was permitted in worship, as though their first obligation was to discover and replicate precise biblical models. However, there is no question but that they believed in the importance of thinking carefully and theologically about every aspect of Lord's Day worship. Presuming that this priority was widely shared, one can understand how the assembly might trust local ministers and church officers to tailor their liturgies to local contexts and sensibilities, guided by the rubrics of their Directory rather than by fixed liturgical texts.

American worship practices, however, have been shaped more by pragmatic than by theological considerations. The need to evangelize the frontier, the successive "awakenings," and the tent-meeting "revival" tradition have shifted the focus of worship to an instrumentalist one, in which worship serves the purpose of making converts or arousing worshippers to a fresh commitment to the gospel. Even in those churches for which the evangelism/revival model is not dominant, there remains the instrumentalist sense that what matters in worship is what "works," and what "works" is whatever draws a crowd and keeps them coming. The pragmatic tradition, then, has no settled practice of thinking theologically about the details of worship. In fact, concern for the details may even be taken as a lack of zeal for building up the church.

The Directory tradition, supplying rubrics for services to be worked out locally, does not serve the church as well under conditions in which pragmatism takes priority over theological considerations. Attentiveness to local sensibilities may easily lead to the neglect or intentional setting aside of liturgical forms that have played a major role in shaping the church's understanding of who God is and who we are as the people of God. While that risk holds true for the whole liturgy, it is particularly evident when forms of eucharistic prayer have become a matter of indifference. All the more reason to resort to the classical eucharistic *ordo*, which does not permit the avoidance of its sometimes difficult biblical affirmations, without which theology and piety will surely be distorted in deference to the prevailing culture. In other words, the *ordo* may serve as a counterweight to local and temporal theological idiosyncrasies.

As the form and content of eucharistic prayer began to evolve historically, the developed forms of that prayer served to give voice to the church's faith in the God of Israel and the church—the God whose story is rendered in Scripture and whom the church has come to know as Holy Trinity. As eucharistic prayer articulates the faith of the church, it also exhibits the content of that faith and at the same time shapes our piety. "Lex orandi, lex credendi"—as we pray, so shall we believe, with the understanding that believing is not simply a matter for the intellect, but also a disposition of the heart and the whole person.

Like the ecumenical creeds, eucharistic prayer not only sets before us those basic biblical affirmations with which Christians always and everywhere have to do, but it also serves a doxological purpose. Classical eucharistic prayer cries out the church's thanksgiving to God, boldly naming the reasons for which it is thankful.

One example of a contemporary eucharistic prayer is Great Thanksgiving A in the Presbyterian (U.S.A.) and Cumberland Presbyterian *Book of Common Worship* (1993).[1] (See Appendix H.) It follows the ecumenical and Antiochene model for eucharistic prayer, beginning with the traditional opening dialogue.

> The Lord be with you.
> **And also with you.**
> Lift up your hearts.
> **We lift them to the Lord.**
> Let us give thanks to the Lord our God.
> **It is right to give our thanks and praise.**

THE PREFACE

The prayer continues with *"It is truly right and our greatest joy to give you thanks and praise . . . ,"* continuing what has traditionally been identified as the Preface with a recital of causes for gratitude, beginning with creation. It is God who created and rules the universe. *"In your wisdom, you made all things and sustain them by your power."* In the Old Testament, Wisdom (or *Sophia*, to use the Greek of the Septuagint) sometimes functions linguistically in a way similar to that in which the New Testament, particularly the Gospel of John, uses the Greek word *logos*. The personification of Wisdom is particularly evident in apocryphal books, but not in them exclusively. The book of Proverbs speaks of Wisdom in personal terms in the section that begins, "Wisdom cries out in the street; in the squares she raises her voice" (Prov. 1:20). Even in the New Testament one may find allusions to Wisdom used in this way. For example, Luke writes, "Therefore also *the Wisdom of God* says, 'I will send them prophets and apostles, some of whom they will kill and persecute'" (Luke 11:49, italics added). God's "sophia" (Wisdom), or God's "logos" (Word) name the agents by which God created the universe.

In the twenty-first century, when people in our culture often seem to feel themselves adrift, without a story to tell, coming from nowhere in particular and headed to oblivion, it is more than commonplace to identify God not only as the source of all things, but as the One by whom everything is held together. Against the forces of nihilism, the church declares that the universe is not the result of random chance, but has its origin in the purpose and intention of God, and that God has not abandoned the project.

The Preface continues, *"You formed us in your image . . ."* The twentieth and twenty-first centuries have witnessed a series of atrocities: Armenian genocide; the Holocaust; Hiroshima; wartime massacres in southeast Asia; mass killings in Rwanda; suicide bombers and other indiscriminate killings and humiliations carried out in God's name or even in the name of "freedom," to name only a few. It is all too easy to hold "the other" in contempt, whether the other is of another race, another religion, another nationality, or another political conviction. The prayer affirms the biblical faith that there is no human person whose being is not stamped with the image of God. Human life may be plentiful, but nevertheless it may not be wasted or denied the respect with which God has endowed it.

". . . setting us in this world to love and to serve you . . ." Human life has a purpose. We have not simply been thrown up on this shore by accident, to be washed away again as the tides come and go. And the purpose of human life has to do with love, a word overused in our society, or trivialized, but a word with profound meaning when it is understood to be rooted in God's own love

for the creation. In human life, the created world, conceived in love, comes to consciousness and becomes capable of returning love for love and translating that love into practical action. We are here for God and one another.

"*. . . and to live in peace with your whole creation.*" The prayer reminds us that the creation is first of all God's, and that since it is God's possession, it requires to be cared for rather than mindlessly exploited. Given the ecological crises of which we have become aware in our time, it has become more urgent than ever to think theologically about human responsibility toward the creation, understanding that the dominion God has given to us is a stewardship obligation rather than a license to plunder. Such responsibility is rooted in the doctrine of creation that acknowledges the continuing sovereignty of God.

At this point, the Preface of Great Thanksgiving A rehearses the main outline of the Old Testament story, from Genesis through the prophets. Human beings "rebelled." Yet, even when we refused to trust and obey our Creator, God did not abandon us, "*but still claimed us as your own.*" And how did God continue to hold on to us, even though we tried over and over to escape the divine hand? "*You sent prophets to call us back to your way.*" Though they are not named, we may recall Elijah, Jeremiah, Isaiah, Amos, Joel, and a host of others who endured contempt and hardship in faithfulness to the divine calling that, like fire in the bones, they could not extinguish. Again and again God refused to let go of us, repeatedly calling out to us in our rebellion and indifference, directing us away from the ways of death and toward the way that leads to life. And at last, "*out of your great love for the world, you sent your only Son to be one of us, to redeem us and heal our brokenness.*"

The recital of God's care for us, having reached its climactic moment in the incarnation, moves toward the singing of Sanctus, introduced by the Pre-Sanctus: "*Therefore we praise you, joining our voices with choirs of angels, with prophets, apostles, and martyrs, and with all the faithful of every time and place.*"

Who are these "angels"? The prayer invokes angels along with God's servants who have borne faithful witness, not to teach a doctrine about unseen beings, but to evoke the great chorus of heavenly song with which our mortal voices are joined. The whole creation, that part of it which we know by sight and those parts of it which are invisible and unknown to us, joins the song of praise:

> *Holy, holy, holy Lord, God of power and might,*
> *heaven and earth are full of your glory.*
> *Hosanna in the highest.*
>
> *Blessed is he who comes in the name of the Lord.*
> *Hosanna in the highest.*

In the singing of the Sanctus and the Benedictus, the voices of the whole congregation join with the voice of the presider, as well as with the voices of unseen hosts, claiming the prayer as their own in a great doxological outpouring.

THE POST-SANCTUS (ANAMNESIS)

The classical eucharistic prayer must be understood as unitary, that is, as one complete, undivided prayer. In fact, we should understand that the liturgy as a whole, in its entirety, from the moment of gathering to the final benediction comprises the eucharistic action, rather than thinking of that action as reduced to one or more isolated parts, whether Words of Institution, or Epiclesis, or even the anaphora as such, from the opening dialogue to the Lord's Prayer. The Sanctus and Benedictus bring to a conclusion the first part of the tripartite eucharistic prayer, the Preface that focuses on God the Father, and provide a transition into the second part of the prayer, which turns toward God's redemptive acts in Jesus Christ.

While the entire prayer is addressed to the Father, the second movement particularly celebrates what God has done for us in Christ. Traditionally, this part of the eucharistic prayer has been called the Post-Sanctus, although it may also be identified as the Anamnesis (memory, remembering, or memorial), since it recalls the story of Jesus Christ.

"You are holy, O God of majesty, and blessed is Jesus Christ, your Son, our Lord." Poetically and doxologically, the assembly, by means of its prayer, thanks God for the incarnation and for Jesus' ministry, naming especially his work of healing the sick, feeding the hungry, opening the eyes of the blind, sharing table fellowship *"with outcasts and sinners,"* and proclaiming the kingdom to *"the poor and needy."* This second part of the prayer specifically mentions *"Jesus, born of Mary."* Mary's role and status are not defined, but neither is she forgotten. Clearly, this part of the prayer celebrates the humanity of Jesus, born of woman into the same complicated world into which we are born.

The recital of God's redemptive work in Christ moves forward to cross, self-oblation, resurrection, victory over death, session at the right hand of the Father, and promise to come again *"to make all things new."* To name these things takes only a few words, but how crucial they are! Particularly in their Eucharists, Reformed and most other Western churches have tended to focus on the cross and Jesus' offering of himself, while the resurrection has been treated in a disconnected way, as though it were no more than the last chapter of the Jesus story, in which God vindicates Jesus and demonstrates his authority to believers, bringing the gospel story to its conclusion with the promise of eternal life to those who have faith. Although Reformed have frequently celebrated Christ's ascension and his reigning "in glory," accenting his sovereignty in all things, at the same time, more often than not, we have muted the eschatological hope of his coming again, even while we declare with the creed: "He will come again to judge the living and the dead."

The resurrection is not, after all, the last chapter in Jesus' story. Rather, it serves as God's solemn promise of a cosmic redemption, a new heaven and earth. The resurrection doesn't finish something, but points forward to a fresh beginning, the Parousia, the coming kingdom. The church as a whole, excepting the Orthodox, has backed away from eschatological themes, and when it speaks at all of the kingdom or reign of God, it has tended to interpret it in reduced terms. In some definitions, the kingdom is simply another way of speaking of the church, the community in which Christ's lordship is acknowledged. In other definitions, the kingdom is a way of speaking of "heaven," the ultimate refuge of the faithful, which receives us one by one after our deaths. Or the kingdom is something that Christians are supposed to build by their determination and effort. But the meaning of "kingdom of heaven" in Jesus' preaching is far more nuanced, and yet at the same time far more specific, than the church, or eternal life, or a human improvement project. While it is "among us," becoming manifest to human experience now here, now there, but beyond our control or ability to predict, the reign of God is also "not yet," referring to the ultimate consummation in which "all flesh shall see the salvation of God" (Luke 3:6, quoting Isa. 40:5).

The Eucharist itself, as Alexander Schmemann argues, is a manifestation of the kingdom. As Christ himself is, in a sense, the kingdom made present in human history, so then, wherever Christ is, the kingdom is. Christ is present in Word and Sacrament; thus, in the Eucharist understood as the entire liturgy of Word and Sacrament, Christ, and therefore the kingdom, becomes manifest. When we discern and celebrate the kingdom made manifest in the Eucharist, we are better equipped to discern signs of it in our midst in the doings of people and nations, and so to lend our energies to that which may lead to its further manifestation, while at the same time investing our hope in a redemption played out on a large screen—a cosmic redemption—hope for the whole creation and not just for a few making their way to "heaven" one by one.

By muting the eschatological themes of Scripture, Reformed and most Western churches have left a vacuum that has been filled by those who take those themes out of context and distort them, sometimes using the eschatological promise as a weapon to terrify, threaten, or punish. The ecumenical church must recover a bold proclamation of the kingdom that does not lend itself to sectarian distortion, and such proclamation must take liturgical as well as discursive forms. When eucharistic prayer consistently lifts up, in a doxological fashion, the promise of the reign of God, that glad promise will be more likely to find a lodging in the hearts and minds of the assembly.[2]

At this point, the Post-Sanctus typically begins the institution narrative, as does Great Thanksgiving A. *"We give you thanks that the Lord Jesus, on the night before he died, took bread . . ."* As noted above, the ecumenical tradition has been to use the *verba* here, while the Reformed have more typically taken them out of the anaphora and used them either before or after it. One reason for the Reformed usage is that the institution narrative, as Calvin insisted, is clearly addressed to the church, and not to God. By marking the *verba* in brackets, Great Thanksgiving A offers the option of using them within the prayer or outside of it. The rubric reads, "If they have not already been said, the words of institution may be said here, or in relation to the breaking of the bread."

A way of using the institution narrative in an ecumenical way, while perhaps even satisfying objections such as Calvin's, might be to consider the way the *verba* have been used in the eucharistic liturgy of the Church of South India. The CSI liturgy, following the example of the ancient Liturgy of St. James, uses the institution narrative in its chronologically appropriate position within the recital of specific things God has done for us in Christ, which the church names as causes for thanksgiving. The institution narrative *follows* mention of Christ's incarnation, but *precedes* specific mention of his death, resurrection, ascension, and coming again. Following that model, a eucharistic prayer similar to Great Thanksgiving A might give thanks, in this order, for: incarnation, earthly ministry, *institution of the Lord's Supper*, cross, resurrection, ascension, session at God's right hand, coming again to inaugurate the consummation of the kingdom.

Whether or not the institution narrative is used within the prayer, the Post-Sanctus moves toward that portion of it that, technically and in the strictest sense, has been identified as the Anamnesis (remembering). *"Remembering your gracious acts in Jesus Christ, we take from your creation this bread and wine and joyfully celebrate his dying and rising, as we await the day of his coming."* At this point, the prayer once again separates the church's faith from that of gnostics and Docetists and all others who denigrate the physical world, as though "spiritual" and "material" were incompatible. The prayer also reiterates the church's faith in Christ as the one who died and rose from the dead and whose glory shall be revealed at the consummation of the reign of God.

The Post-Sanctus concludes with what has traditionally been called the "oblation." *"With thanksgiving, we offer our very selves to you to be a living and holy sacrifice, dedicated to your service."* Then, bringing together Roman and early Eastern practice, there follow four alternative congregational acclamations.

1 *Great is the mystery of faith.*　　2 *Praise to you, Lord Jesus:*
Christ has died,　　　　　　　　**Dying, you destroyed our death,**
Christ is risen,　　　　　　　　**rising you restored our life.**
Christ will come again.　　　　**Lord Jesus, come in glory.**

3 *According to his commandment:*　4 *Christ is the bread of life:*
We remember his death,　　　　**When we eat this bread and drink this cup,**
we proclaim his resurrection,　**we proclaim your death, Lord Jesus,**
we await his coming in glory.　**until you come in glory.**

All four reinforce the eucharistic themes that are, in fact, the gospel: Christ has died, is risen, will come again.

THE EPICLESIS

The third part of this Trinitarian (tripartite) prayer, traditionally called the Epiclesis, asks God to *"pour out your Holy Spirit upon us and upon these your gifts of bread and wine."* The emergence of Pentecostal churches and of charismatic movements in the past century may serve as a rebuke to the historic churches of the West, in which the Holy Spirit has often been neglected. Once again, the classic form of the anaphora serves to remind us of the church's full Trinitarian faith, which certainly calls for both a theology and a piety not only of the Father and of the Son, but also of the Holy Spirit.

Whereas the new Roman eucharistic prayers typically separate this petition into two separate and distinct Epicleses, one before the institution narrative and one after, the Antiochene form combines them, as does Great Thanksgiving A, in this position after the *verba*, joining the petition that the Spirit may bless the *community* with petition that the same Spirit may be "poured out" upon the *gifts*. The Epiclesis does not attempt to define eucharistic "consecration" in metaphysical terms (nor does it use the word), but it does boldly petition God *"that the bread we break and the cup we bless may be the communion of the body and blood of Christ."*

Calvin's theology of the Eucharist relies so heavily on the Holy Spirit that it would seem that Reformed churches ought never to neglect the Epiclesis in their eucharistic prayer, and in written texts, they rarely do. Theologically, use of the Epiclesis is fundamental to our Reformed as well as to our ecumenical identity, particularly as it links us to the Orthodox, as Calvin's eucharistic theology also linked him.

The Epiclesis continues, asking that the Spirit might unite us with Christ (again, a major theme in Calvin) and with one another, that we may be *"united in ministry in every place.*" The prayer then links the Spirit's work of manifesting Christ's "body" in the bread with the Spirit's action to manifest the church as "body of Christ," asking that God send us out *"to be the body of Christ in the world."* Our faith, then, is not merely a luxury for the church to enjoy apart from any concern for the created world or for the neighbor, for whose sake the people of God have been chosen and to whom they have been sent.

Eastern prayers often included intercessions within the body of the eucharistic prayer following the Epiclesis, and Great Thanksgiving A offers the option of following that example. Ordinarily, *"intercessions for the church and the world,"* sometimes called the Prayers of the People, the Prayers of the Church, or the Pastoral Prayer, follow the sermon and precede the offering, but they may be included here. In practice, unfortunately, it is not uncommon in Reformed churches for intercessions to be entirely omitted on Communion Sundays, perhaps because of anxiety about the length of the service. Omitting prayers of intercession is never good practice. Among other things, such omission distorts the church's understanding of itself and its mission as "royal priesthood" (1 Pet. 2:9). Offering these prayers within the eucharistic prayer, after the Epiclesis, is an option.

The traditional Antiochene prayers conclude with remembrance of the saints and all the blessed departed. Great Thanksgiving A prays, *"In union with your church in heaven and on earth, we pray, O God, that you will fulfill your eternal purpose in us and in all the world."* Remembrance of the faithful departed continues in the next line, *"Keep us faithful in your service until Christ comes in final victory"* (once again, the eschatological theme is lifted up), *"and we shall feast with all your saints in the joy of your eternal realm."* The reference to feasting evokes the messianic banquet, an image of the kingdom or reign of God, when, according to Luke, people "will come from east and west, and from north and south, and eat in the kingdom of God" (Luke 13:29). Thus the prayer draws toward a conclusion on a note of joy, promise, and expectation.

The concluding Trinitarian doxology is typical of eucharistic prayers both East and West. *"Through Christ, with Christ, in Christ, in the unity of the Holy Spirit, all glory and honor are yours, almighty Father, now and forever."* The people sing (or say) the Great Amen, voicing their affirmation of the prayer uttered on behalf of all by the presider, just as Justin Martyr described the people's Amen when writing his description of the Eucharist in the second century. Once again, following practice that has become universal, the prayer concludes with the Lord's Prayer. Great Thanksgiving A offers three optional introductions:

1. Let us pray for God's rule on earth as Jesus taught us:
2. And now, with the confidence of the children of God, let us pray:
3. As our Savior Christ has taught us, we are bold to pray.

DO HISTORICAL MODELS MATTER?

Do contemporary Presbyterians and other Christians *have* to follow ecumenical models, as do the Great Thanksgivings in the *Book of Common Worship*? Certainly there is no *must* about it. The Reformed tradition has no history of judgments about what makes a sacrament valid or what omissions make it invalid. We have not been accustomed to thinking of sacramental actions in legal terms. The ways that Christian assemblies have prayed the Eucharist in times past serve us not as a law to be obeyed under threat of some penalty, but as a gift to be received. To pray the Eucharist guided by the experience of the greater church links us not only with apostles and martyrs and the whole communion of saints, but also with Jesus of Nazareth and with the people of Israel, whose tradition nurtured him. It also simply makes sense that such prayer would offer praise and thanks to God, the creator of the world and giver of life, and recall the stories of God's redemptive activity among us; that our prayer should give thanks for Jesus Christ, his incarnation and birth, his life and ministry, his death, resurrection, ascension, and the eschatological promise of his coming again; and that we should offer our petition, asking God, by the Holy Spirit, to bless us and the sacramental actions.

Different patterns of eucharistic prayer developed in the East, with its focus on the Epiclesis, and the West, with its focus on the Words of Institution, but contemporary historical, liturgical, and theological study has led toward a consensus that includes the treasures of both East and West. For Reformed Christians, a crucial question may be, Are we a sect, or are we a part of the church catholic? In other words, does our eucharistic praying slavishly imitate the patterns set by the Reformers, whose prayer was shaped in response to specific controversies of their time, or do we follow the Reformers more faithfully when we search out the best interests of gospel and church for this moment? Put another way, do the larger church and its tradition have anything to say about how we pray, or do we owe a debt only to our own confessional precedents?

Some might argue that maintaining denominational or confessional distinctiveness takes priority over other considerations, so that, whatever their deficiencies, it would be better for Reformed to use Calvin's prayer, or Bucer's, or John Knox's. However, even the Westminster Assembly, in composing the first Directory for Worship, believed that it was possible to make improvements on the eucharistic prayers already known to them. If Reformed distinctiveness were to trump other considerations, choosing which Reformed model to follow would still pose a problem. In any case, Reformed have not typically considered confessional distinctiveness to be an ultimate value. Reformed have not aspired to some sort of sectarian superiority, but rather have chosen to function as active participants in the church catholic, both offering their own gifts and welcoming the gifts of others. Particularly in this post-Christendom era, sectarian consciousness undermines the evangelical testimony of the church. It is far better to look for every possible way to signal the church's essential unity in Christ. Only in serious matters of conscience ought we to go our own way.

The sixteenth General Council of the (former) World Presbyterian Alliance (1948) stated that

> in liturgy, as in doctrine, the Reformed Church recognizes as normative—as absolutely binding—only what is revealed by the Word of God contained in our Bible. . . . In liturgy, as in doctrine, the Reformed Church cannot recognize tradition as a second normative authority alongside the Bible. Therefore, she admits variety of liturgical forms in everything that is not fixed by scripture. But, in liturgy as in doctrine, the Reformed Church respects tradition as a consultative authority. Her liberty in all that is not fixed by the Word of God permits her therefore to preserve or to recover all traditional elements that are not clearly anti-evangelical. She is favourably disposed towards tradition, until compelled to dissent by proof to the contrary because her aim is not to be anti-catholic but pro-evangelical.[3]

The point of embracing models of eucharistic prayer representing an ecumenical consensus is not based on a presumption that we must reproduce an idealized formula from the past, whether dating from the sixteenth century, the twelfth, the third, or even the first. Nor is the point to assess "validity," as though our eucharists were occasions for legal assessment and adjudication rather than doxological. The point, rather, is to give thanks, and bless, and petition in a confessionally Trinitarian way; to honor the God who created the world and all life within it; who has redeemed, is redeeming, and will redeem us in Christ's incarnation, ministry, death, resurrection, ascension, and coming again; and who draws near to us by the power of the Holy Spirit in bread taken, blessed, broken, and given, and in the cup of blessing. Such prayer is most certainly both catholic and evangelical.

The eucharistic prayer, like the liturgy as a whole, is not the possession of clergy alone, or of single congregations alone, or even of denominations alone. It belongs to the whole church. If we are truly catholic rather than sectarian, then every Christian should expect to hear whenever she or he is present at the Eucharist in a Reformed church not just the Words of Institution, or an ordinary table grace, or an explanation of sacramental doctrine in place of prayer, or yet a pastoral prayer with allusion to the meal, but rather prayer recognizable as the eucharistic prayer of the whole church—certainly Trinitarian in its form, and doxological in its character.

Appendix A

Martin Bucer's Eucharistic Prayer (the third of three alternatives)

This prayer is the latter part of the intercessory prayer that follows Sermon, Explanation of the Supper, Words of Institution, and Creed. It is not an embolism, but a regular part of the prayer, presuming that weekly Eucharist is the norm. The prayer begins with a dialogue between minister and people:

The Lord be with you.
And also with you.

Almighty God and heavenly Father . . .

And may all of us, here gathered before you, in the name of your Son and at your table, O God and Father, truly and profoundly acknowledge the sin and depravity in which we were born, and into which we thrust ourselves more and more deeply by our sinful life. And since there is nothing good in our flesh, indeed since our flesh and blood cannot inherit your kingdom, grant that we may yield ourselves with all our hearts in true faith to your Son, our only Redeemer and Savior. And since, for our sake, he has not only offered his body and blood upon the cross to you for our sin, but also wishes to give them to us for food and drink unto eternal life, grant that we may accept his goodness and gift with complete longing and devotion, and faithfully partake of and enjoy his true Body and true Blood—even himself, our Savior, true God and true man, the only true bread from heaven; so that we may live no more in our sins and depravity, but that he may live in us and we in him—a holy, blessed and eternal life, verily partaking of the true and eternal testament, the covenant of grace, in sure confidence that you will be our gracious Father forever, never again reckoning our sins against us, and in all things providing for us in body and soul, as your heirs and dear children: so that we may at all times give thanks and praise, and glorify your holy name in all that we say and do. Wherefore, heavenly Father, grant that we may celebrate today the glorious and blessed memorial of your dear Son our Lord and proclaim his death, so that we shall continually grow and increase in faith to you and in all goodness. So, in sure confidence we call upon you now and always, God and Father, and pray as our Lord taught us to pray, saying: Our Father . . .

_____

R. C. D. Jasper and G. J. Cuming, *Prayers of the Eucharist: Early and Reformed* (Collegeville, MN: Liturgical Press, 1990), 210.

Appendix B

John Calvin's Eucharistic Prayer (and Exhortation)

On days when the Lord's Supper was to be celebrated, Calvin added this eucharistic embolism to the prayers of intercession that normally followed the sermon.

And as our Lord Jesus has not only offered His body and blood once on the Cross for the remission of our sins, but also desires to impart them to us as our nourishment unto everlasting life, grant us this grace: that we may receive at His hands such a great benefit and gift with true sincerity of heart and with ardent zeal. In steadfast faith may we receive His body and blood, yea Christ Himself entire, who being true God and true man, is verily the holy bread and heaven which gives us life. So may we live no longer in ourselves, after our nature which is entirely corrupt and vicious, but may He live in us and lead us to the life that is holy, blessed and everlasting: whereby we may truly become partakers of the new and eternal testament, the covenant of grace, assured that it is thy good pleasure to be our gracious Father forever, never reckoning our faults against us, and to provide for us, as thy well-beloved children and heirs, all our needs both of body and soul. Thus may we render praise and thanks unto thee without ceasing and magnify thy name in word and deed.

Grant us, therefore, O heavenly Father, so to celebrate this day the blessed memorial and remembrance of thy dear Son, to exercise ourselves in the same, and to proclaim the benefit of His death, that, receiving new growth and strength in faith and in all things good, we may with so much greater confidence proclaim thee our Father and glory in thee. Amen.

Bard Thompson, *Liturgies of the Western Church* (Philadelphia: Fortress Press, 1961), 202.

At every celebration of the Lord's Supper, Calvin also included an exhortation addressed to the congregation. Many subsequent Reformed liturgies followed his example.

Let us listen to the institution of the Holy Supper by Jesus Christ, as narrated by St. Paul in the eleventh chapter of the first epistle to the Corinthians.

For I have received, he says, from the Lord what I also delivered to you, that the Lord Jesus, on the night when he was betrayed, took bread, and when he had given thanks, he broke it, and said, This is my body, which is broken for you. Do this in remembrance of me. In the same way also he took the cup, after supper, saying, This cup is the new covenant in my blood. Do this, as oft as you drink it, in remembrance of me. For as often as you eat this bread and drink this cup, you will proclaim the Lord's death until he comes. Whoever, therefore, eats the bread or drinks the cup of the Lord in an unworthy manner will be guilty of the body and blood of the Lord. Let a man examine himself, and so eat of this bread and drink of this cup. For anyone who eats and drinks unworthily incurs condemnation, not discerning the Lord's body.

We have heard, brethren, how our Lord celebrated his Supper with his disciples, thereby indicating that strangers, and those who are not of the company of the faithful, ought not to be admitted. Therefore, in accordance with this rule, in the name and by the authority of our Lord Jesus Christ, I excommunicate all idolators, blasphemers, despisers of God, heretics, and all who form private sects to break the unity of the Church, all perjurers, all who rebel against parents or their superiors, all who are seditious, mutinous, quarrelsome or brutal, all adulterers, fornicators, thieves, ravishers, misers, drunkards, gluttons, and all who lead a scandalous and dissolute life. I declare that they must abstain from this holy table, for fear of defiling and contaminating the holy food which our Lord Jesus Christ gives only to his household and believers.

Therefore, in accordance with the exhortation of St. Paul, let each man prove and examine his conscience, to see whether he has truly repented of his faults, and is dissatisfied with his sins, desiring to live henceforth a holy life and according to God. Above all, let each man see whether he puts his trust in the mercy of God, and seeks his salvation entirely in Jesus Christ; and whether, renouncing all hatred and rancor, he truly intends and resolves to live in peace and brotherly love with his neighbors.

If we have this testimony in our hearts before God, let us have no doubt at all that he claims us for his children, and that the Lord Jesus addresses his words to us, to invite us to his table, and to present to us this holy sacrament which he communicated to his disciples.

And although we may feel within ourselves much frailty and misery from not having perfect faith, but being inclined to unbelief and distrust; from not being devoted to the service of God so entirely and with such zeal as we ought, but having to war daily against the lusts of our own flesh; nevertheless, since our Lord has graciously permitted us to have his gospel imprinted on our hearts, in order to withstand all unbelief, and has given us the desire and longing to renounce our own desires, in order to follow righteousness and his holy commandments, let us all be assured that the sins and imperfections which remain in us will not prevent him from receiving us, and making us worthy to partake of this spiritual table: for we do not come to declare that we are perfect or righteous in ourselves; but, on the contrary, by seeking our life in Christ, we confess that we are in death. Let us therefore understand that this sacrament is a medicine for the spiritually poor and sick, and that the only worthiness which our Savior requires in us is to know ourselves, so as to be dissastisfied with our vices, and have all our pleasure, joy and contentment in him alone.

First, then, let us believe in those promises which Jesus Christ, who is the unfailing truth, has pronounced with his own lips, namely, that he is indeed willing to make us partakers of his own body and blood, in order that we may possess him entirely and in such a manner that he may live in us, and we in him. And although we see only bread and wine, yet let us not doubt that he accomplishes spiritually in our souls all that he shows us outwardly by these visible signs; in other words, that he is heavenly bread, to feed and nourish us unto eternal life.

Next, let us not be unmindful of the infinite goodness of our Savior, who displays all his riches and blessings at this table, in order to give them to us; for, in giving himself to us, he bears testimony to us that all which he has is ours. Moreover, let us receive this sacrament as a pledge that the virtue of his death and Passion is imputed to us for righteousness, just as if we had suffered it in our own persons. Let us never be so perverse as to hold back when Jesus Christ invites us so gently by his word. But, reflecting on the dignity of the precious gift which he gives us, let us present ourselves to him with ardent zeal, in order that he may make us capable of receiving him.

With this in mind, let us raise our hearts and minds on high, where Jesus Christ is, in the glory of his Father, and from whence we look for him at our redemption. Let us not be bemused by these earthly and corruptible elements which we see with the eye, and touch with the hand, in order to seek him there, as if he were enclosed in the bread or wine. Our souls will only then be disposed to be nourished and vivified by his substance, when they are thus raised above all earthly things, and carried as high as heaven, to enter the kingdom of God where he dwells. Let us therefore be content to have the bread and the wine as signs and evidences, spiritually seeking the reality where the word of God promises that we shall find it.

_____

R. C. D. Jasper and G. J. Cuming, *Prayers of the Eucharist: Early and Reformed* (Collegeville, MN: Liturgical Press, 1990), 215 ff.

Appendix C

The Roman Canon

This is a literal translation of the Latin prototype. Vernacular translations must be approved by the Vatican. The Sacramentary uses the ICEL (International Consultation on English in the Liturgy) version of the canon. After the opening dialogue and the Proper Preface, the Canon continues:

Therefore, most merciful Father, we humbly beg and entreat you through Jesus Christ your Son, our Lord, to accept and bless these gifts, these offerings, these holy and spotless sacrifices which we offer you first for your holy catholic Church, that you may grant her peace and protection, unity and direction throughout the world, together with your servant N., our Holy Father, and N., our bishop, and all faithful guardians of the catholic and apostolic faith.

Remember, Lord, your servants N. and N., and all here present, whose faith and devotion are known to you: for whom we offer, or who themselves offer, to you this sacrifice of praise, in their own behalf and in behalf of all who are theirs, for the redemption of their souls, for the hope of their salvation and protection from harm, and who now offer their promises to you, the eternal, living, and true God.

In the unity of holy fellowship, and venerating the memory, first of all, of the glorious and ever-virgin Mary, Mother of our God and Lord, Jesus Christ, then blessed Joseph, spouse of that same virgin, your blessed apostles and martyrs Peter and Paul, Andrew, [James, John, Thomas, James, Philip, Bartholomew, Matthew, Simon, and Thaddeus; Linus, Cletus, Clement, Sixtus, Cornelius, Cyprian, Lawrence, Chrysogonus, John and Paul, Cosmas and Damian;] and all of your saints, through whose merits and prayers grant that we may be ever strengthened by the help of your protection. [Through the same Christ our Lord. Amen.]

We therefore beg you to accept, O Lord, this offering of our worship and that of your whole household. Regulate the days of our lives so that they may be spent in your peace; spare us from eternal damnation and help us to be numbered among those whom you have chosen. [Through Christ our Lord. Amen.]

We pray you, O God, be pleased to make this offering wholly blessed, to consecrate and approve it, making it reasonable and acceptable, so that it may become for us the body and blood of your most beloved Son, our Lord Jesus Christ.

Who, on the day before he suffered death, took bread into his holy and venerable hands, and lifting up his eyes to heaven, to you, O God, his almighty Father, and giving thanks to you, he said the blessing, broke it, and gave it to his disciples, saying: "Take this, all of you, and eat of it: for this is my body, which will be given up for you."

In like manner, after they had eaten, taking this noble cup into his holy and venerable hands, and again giving thanks to you, he said the blessing, and gave it to his disciples, saying: "Take this, all of you, and drink of it: for this is the cup of my blood of the new and everlasting covenant, which shall be shed for you and for the many for the forgiveness of sins. Do this in memory of me."

The mystery of faith!—Lord, we proclaim your death and we confess your resurrection, until you come.

Therefore, O Lord, we your servants and with us your holy people, calling to mind the blessed passion of this same Christ, your Son, our Lord, and also his resurrection from the dead and his glorious ascension into heaven, offer to your supreme majesty, of the gifts you have bestowed on us, a pure, holy, and spotless sacrifice, the holy bread of everlasting life and the cup of eternal salvation.

Be pleased to look upon these offerings with a gracious and kindly countenance, and accept them as it pleased you to accept the offerings of your just servant Abel, and the sacrifice of our father Abraham, and that which your great priest Melchizedek offered to you, a holy sacrifice, a spotless offering.

Humbly we implore you, almighty God, bid these offerings be carried by the hands of your holy angel to your altar on high, before your divine majesty, so that those of us who by sharing in the sacrifice at this altar shall receive the sacred body and blood of your Son, may be filled with every grace and heavenly blessing. [Through the same Christ our Lord. Amen.]

Remember also, O Lord, your servants N. and N., who have gone before us with the sign of faith, and rest in the sleep of peace. To them, O Lord, and to all who rest in Christ, we entreat you to grant a place of comfort, light, and peace. [Through Christ our Lord. Amen.]

To us also, your sinful servants, who trust in your boundless mercy, graciously grant fellowship and a place with your holy apostles and martyrs, with John, Stephen, Matthias, Barnabas, [Ignatius, Alexander, Marcellinus, Peter, Felicity, Perpetua, Agatha, Lucy, Agnes, Cecilia, Anastasia,] and all your saints. Into their company we beg you, admit us, not weighing our unworthiness but freely grant us forgiveness.

Through Christ our Lord, through whom, O Lord, you constantly create, sanctify, enliven, and bestow upon us all these good gifts.

Through him and with him and in him all honor and glory is yours, almighty God and Father, in the unity of the Holy Spirit, for ever and ever. Amen.

Enrico Mazza, *The Eucharistic Prayers of the Roman Rite* (New York: Pueblo Publishing Co., 1986), 49.

Appendix D

John Knox's Eucharistic Prayer

O Father of mercy and God of all consolation,
seeing all creatures do acknowledge and confess thee,
as governor and lord, it becometh us the workmanship
of thine own hands, at all times to reverence and magnify
thy godly majesty, first that thou hast created us to thine
own image and similitude: but chiefly that thou hast
delivered us, from that everlasting death and damnation
into the which Satan drew mankind by the means of sin:
from the bondage whereof neither man nor angel was
able to make us free, but thou, O Lord, rich in mercy and
infinite in goodness, hast provided our redemption to stand
in thy only and well-beloved son: whom of very love
thou didst give to be made man, like unto us in all things,
sin except, that in his body he might receive the
punishments of our transgression, by his death to make
satisfaction to thy justice, and by his resurrection to destroy
him that was the author of death, and so to reduce and bring
again life to the world, from which the whole offspring of
Adam most justly was exiled.

O Lord, we acknowledge that no creature is able to
comprehend the length and breadth, the deepness and
height, of that thy most excellent love which moved thee
to show mercy, where none was deserved; to promise and
give life, where death had gotten victory; but to receive us

into thy grace, when we would do nothing but rebel against
thy justice.

O Lord, the blind dullness of our corrupt nature will not
suffer us sufficiently to weigh these thy most ample benefits:
yet nevertheless at the commandment of Jesus Christ our
Lord, we present our selves to this his table, which he hath
left to be used in remembrance of his death until his
coming again, to declare and witness before the world, that
by him alone we have received liberty and life: that by him
alone, thou dost acknowledge us thy children and heirs:
that by him alone, we have entrance to the throne of thy
grace: that by him alone, we are possessed in our spiritual
kingdom, to eat and drink at his table: with whom we have
our conversation presently in heaven, and by whom our
bodies shall be raised up again from the dust, and shall be
placed with him in that endless joy, which thou, O father
of mercy, hast prepared for thine elect, before the foundation
of the world was laid.

And these most inestimable benefits, we acknowledge and
confess to have received of thy free mercy and grace, by
thy only beloved Son Jesus Christ, for the which therefore
we thy congregation moved by thy Holy Spirit render thee
all thanks, praise, and glory for ever and ever.

R. C. D. Jasper and G. J. Cuming, *Prayers of the Eucharist: Early and Reformed* (Collegeville, MN: Liturgical Press, 1990), 255.

Appendix E

Eucharistic Prayer in 1906
Book of Common Worship

Invitation
Hymn
Words of Institution

> *Then the Minister shall say,*
> Let us pray.

If so desired, these PRAYERS *and* THANKSGIVINGS *may be offered in the form following; the People reverently bowing down:*
O God, who by the blood of Thy dear Son hast consecrated for us a new and living way into the holiest of all; Cleanse our minds, we beseech Thee, by the inspiration of Thy Holy Spirit, that drawing near unto Thee with a pure heart and undefiled conscience, we may receive these Thy gifts without sin, and worthily magnify Thy holy Name; through Jesus Christ our Lord. *Amen.*

> *Then the People, still bowing down, shall make these responses:*

> Minister: The Lord be with you.
>   People: **And with thy spirit.**
> Minister: Lift up your hearts.
>   People: **We lift them up unto the Lord.**
> Minister: Let us give thanks unto the Lord our God.
>   People: **It is meet and right so to do.**

It is very meet, right, and our bounden duty, that we should, at all times and in all places, give thanks unto Thee, O Lord, Holy Father, Almighty and Eternal God, for all Thy bounties known and unknown; but chiefly are we bound to praise Thee that Thou hast ransomed us from eternal death, and given us the joyful hope of everlasting life through Jesus Christ Thy Son, whom Thou didst send into the world to suffer death upon the cross for our redemption. Thee, God the Father Everlasting: Thee, Only Begotten Son: Thee, Holy Spirit, the Comforter: Holy, Blessed and Glorious Trinity: we confess and praise with heart and mouth; saying, with angels and archangels, and all the company of Heaven,

Here let the People, still bowing down, join aloud, singing or saying,
Holy, Holy, Holy, Lord God of Hosts; Heaven and earth are full of the majesty of Thy glory. Hosanna in the highest. Blessed is He that cometh in the Name of the Lord. Hosanna in the highest.

Then the Minister shall proceed, saying,
    Almighty God, the Father of our Lord Jesus Christ, whose once offering up of Himself, by Himself, upon the cross, once for all, we commemorate before Thee; We beseech Thee to accept this our spiritual oblation of all possible praise for the same. And here we offer and present, O Lord, ourselves, our souls and bodies, to be a reasonable, holy, and living sacrifice, acceptable unto Thee through Jesus Christ Thy Son:
    And we most humbly beseech Thee, Father of all mercies and God of all comfort, to vouchsafe Thy gracious presence, and the effectual working of Thy Spirit in us, and so to sanctify these elements both of Bread and Wine, and to bless Thine own Ordinance; that we may receive by faith Christ crucified for us, and so feed upon Him, that He may be one with us and we with Him; that He may live in us, and we in Him who hath loved us, and given Himself for us:
    Even Jesus Christ our Lord; to whom, with Thee and the Holy Ghost, be praise and power, might, majesty, and dominion, both now and evermore. *Amen.*

———————

The Book of Common Worship, Published by Authority of the General Assembly of the Presbyterian Church in the United States of America (Philadelphia: Presbyterian Board of Publication and Sabbath-School Work, 1906).

Appendix F

The Westminster Directory of 1644

Sermon
Exhortation, Warning, and Invitation
Gathering at the Table
Words of Institution

Let the Prayer, Thanksgiving, or Blessing of the Bread and Wine, be to this effect:

With humble and hearty acknowledgement of the greatness of our misery, from which neither man nor angel was able to deliver us, and of our great unworthiness of the least of all God's mercies; To give thanks to God for all His benefits, and especially for that great benefit of our redemption, the love of God the Father, the sufferings and merits of the Lord Jesus Christ the Son of God, by which we are delivered; and for all means of grace, the Word and Sacraments; and for this Sacrament in particular, by which Christ, and all His benefits, are applied and sealed up unto us, which, notwithstanding the denial of them unto others, are in great mercy continued unto us, after so much and long abuse of them all.

To profess that there is no other name under heaven by which we can be saved, but the Name of Jesus Christ, by whom alone we receive liberty and life, have access to the throne of grace, are admitted to eat and drink at His own Table, and are sealed up by His Spirit to an assurance of happiness and everlasting life.

Earnestly to pray to God, the Father of all mercies, and God of all consolation, to vouchsafe His gracious presence, and the effectual working of His Spirit in us; and so to sanctify these Elements both of Bread and Wine, and to bless His own Ordinance, that we may receive by faith the Body and Blood of Jesus Christ, crucified for us, and so to feed upon Him, that He may be one with us, and we with Him; that He may live in us, and we in Him, and to Him who hath loved us, and given Himself for us.

Thomas Leishman, D.D., *The Westminster Directory* (Edinburgh and London: William Blackwood & Sons, 1901), 46.

Appendix G

Eucharistic Prayer K from the United Church of Canada

This brief prayer offers a concise statement of the important themes of eucharistic pray-ing: praise, thanksgiving, remembrance, offering, invocation of the Spirit, and long-ing for God's reign. The form assumes that the institution narrative would be recited outside the body of the prayer

> We praise you, loving God, for creating all things,
> for making us in your image,
> and for seeking us when we turn from you.
> We thank you for coming to us in Jesus Christ,
> who was faithful even to death on a cross,
> and who lives among us still.
> We share this meal in remembrance of him,
> offering you our lives in praise and thanksgiving.
> Fill us with your Spirit, to make us one in Christ,
> and one in love for you and for all people—
> as in word and deed,
> we seek your reign of peace and justice on earth.
> Glory be to you, eternal God, through Jesus Christ,
> in the power of the Holy Spirit.
> **Amen.**

The prayer continues with The Prayer of Jesus.

Celebrate God's Presence: A Book of Services for The United Church of Canada (Toronto: United Church Publishing House, 2000), 267.

Appendix H

Great Thanksgiving A in 1993
Book of Common Worship

After the Opening Dialogue:

It is truly right and our greatest joy
to give you thanks and praise,
O Lord our God, creator and ruler of the universe.
In your wisdom, you made all things
and sustain them by your power.
You formed us in your image,
setting us in this world to love and to serve you,
and to live in peace with your whole creation.
When we rebelled against you
refusing to trust and obey you,
you did not reject us,
but still claimed us as your own.
You sent prophets to call us back to your way.
Then in the fullness of time,
out of your great love for the world,
you sent your only Son to be one of us,
to redeem us and heal our brokenness.

Therefore we praise you,
joining our voices with choirs of angels,
with prophets, apostles, and martyrs,
and with all the faithful of every time and place,
who forever sing to the glory of your name:

Holy, holy, holy Lord, God of power and might,
heaven and earth are full of your glory.
Hosanna in the highest.

Blessed is he who comes in the name of the Lord.
Hosanna in the highest.

You are holy, O God of majesty,
and blessed is Jesus Christ, your Son, our Lord.
In Jesus, born of Mary, your Word became flesh
and dwelt among us, full of grace and truth.
He lived as one of us, knowing joy and sorrow.
He healed the sick,
fed the hungry,
opened blind eyes,
broke bread with outcasts and sinners,
and proclaimed the good news of your kingdom to the poor and needy.
Dying on the cross,
he gave himself for the life of the world.
Rising from the grave,
He won for us victory over death.
Seated at your right hand,
he leads us to eternal life.
We praise you that Christ now reigns with you in glory,
and will come again to make all things new.

If they have not already been said, the words of institution may be said here, or in relation to the breaking of the bread.

We give you thanks that the Lord Jesus,
on the night before he died, took bread,
and after giving thanks to you,
he broke it, and gave it to his disciples, saying:
Take, eat.
This is my body, given for you.
Do this in remembrance of me.

In the same way he took the cup, saying:
This cup is the new covenant sealed in my blood,
shed for you for the forgiveness of sins.
Whenever you drink it,
do this in remembrance of me.

Remembering your gracious acts in Jesus Christ,
we take from your creation this bread and this wine
and joyfully celebrate his dying and rising,
as we await the day of his coming.
With thanksgiving, we offer our very selves to you
to be a living and holy sacrifice,
dedicated to your service.

1 Great is the mystery of faith:
Christ has died,
Christ is risen,
Christ will come again. (Or options 2, 3, or 4)

Gracious God,
pour out your Holy Spirit upon us
and upon these your gifts of bread and wine,
that the bread we break
and the cup we bless
may be the communion of the body and blood of Christ.
By your Spirit make us one with Christ,
that we may be one with all who share this feast,
united in ministry in every place.
As this bread is Christ's body for us,
send us out to be the body of Christ in the world.

Intercessions for the church and the world may be included here, using
these or similar prayers: (See *BCW*, p. 72, for texts of these prayers)

In union with your church in heaven and on earth,
we pray, O God, that you will fulfill your eternal purpose
in us and in all the world,

Keep us faithful in your service
until Christ comes in final victory,
and we shall feast with all your saints
in the joy of your eternal realm.

Through Christ, with Christ, in Christ,
in the unity of the Holy Spirit,
all glory and honor are yours, almighty Father,
now and forever.
Amen.

Lord's Prayer

Appendix I

Time Line for Reformed Liturgies

1524   Diebold Schwartz's *Teutsche Messe* (Strasbourg)

1525   Zwingli, Zurich; and Oecolampadius, Basel

1525   Bucer's first revision of Schwartz's liturgy

1533   Farel, Geneva (first use of the "Reformed Sursum Corda")

1536   Calvin spells out his liturgical form in the *Institutes*

1539   Bucer's Strasbourg liturgy (Calvin in Strasbourg 1538–41)

1542   Calvin's Genevan Liturgy

1549   Cranmer's first Book of Common Prayer

1550   Huycke translates Genevan Liturgy into English

1552   Cranmer's revised Book of Common Prayer

1556   Knox's Liturgy for Marian exiles published in Geneva

1560   Knox's Genevan Liturgy first in use in Scotland

1562   First Scottish edition of Knox's *Book of Common Order*

1637   "Laud's Liturgy"

1644   Westminster Directory (ratified by Church of Scotland, 1645)

1662   Revised English Book of Common Prayer

1788   First American revision of the Westminster Directory for Worship

1790   First American Book of Common Prayer

1857   Mercersburg *Liturgy*

1864   Charles Shields's *Presbyterian Book of Common Prayer*

1865   (Scottish) Church Service Society organized

1866   *Euchologion*

1906   First American *Book of Common Worship*

Notes

Introduction

1. World Council of Churches, *Baptism, Eucharist and Ministry* (Geneva: World Council of Churches, 1982).
2. Ibid., 16. This description of the eucharistic thanksgiving uses material from the *Baptism, Eucharist and Ministry* document.
3. Cf. Ibid.

Chapter One: Early Eucharistic Prayer

1. Louis Bouyer, *Eucharist: Theology and Spirituality of the Eucharistic Prayer* (Notre Dame, London: University of Notre Dame Press, 1968), 79.
2. Ibid., 80.
3. Ibid., 81. "The Jerusalem Talmud assures us that this dialogue goes back at least to the time of Simon ben Shetah, who lived under Alexander Jannaeus—103 to 67 B.C."
4. Ibid., 83. Thomas Talley suggests that the relatively short *berakoth* (blessings) at the end of the meal might introduce a *todah* (thanksgiving), "the prayer which could accept (as the short *berakah* could not) the expansion—yes, the Anamnesis of the *mirabili Dei*— demanded by that most pregnant moment of their common life and ours, and in that prayer, whose opening *yadah* verb proved definitive for Paul and Luke and Justin and the entire tradition, he [the presider] gave thanks" ("From Berakah to Eucharistia," *Worship* 50:124).
5. Bouyer, *Eucharist*, 83.
6. Talley, "From Berakah to Eucharistia," 136.
7. Bryan D. Spinks, "Beware the Liturgical Horses! An English Interjection on Anaphoral Evolution," *Worship* 59 (May 1985): 219.
8. Bouyer, *Eucharist*, 53.
9. Ibid., 56.
10. Paul F. Bradshaw, ed., *Essays on Early Eastern Eucharistic Prayers* (Collegeville, MN: Liturgical Press, 1997), 9, 10.

11. Philippians 1:3, 6, 9.
12. J. Fitzgerald, trans., *Teaching of the Twelve Apostles* (New York: John B. Alden, 1891), 19. Compare with the blessing over the first cup at Jewish meals: "Blessed be thou, JHWH, our God, King of the universe, who givest us this fruit of the vine." (see n. 1)
13. Ibid., 19, 21.
14. Ibid., 21.
15. Bard Thompson, *Liturgies of the Western Church* (Philadelphia: Fortress Press, 1961), 9.
16. Ibid., 8.
17. Ibid., 6.
18. Enrico Mazza, *The Eucharistic Prayers of the Roman Rite* (New York: Pueblo Publishing Co., 1986), 24.
19. Ibid.
20. Ibid., 25.
21. R. C. D. Jasper and G. J. Cuming, *Prayers of the Eucharist: Early and Reformed* (Collegeville, MN: Liturgical Press, 1990), 31.
22. Ibid., 268.
23. Frank C. Senn, *Christian Liturgy: Catholic and Evangelical* (Minneapolis: Fortress Press, 1997), 79.
24. Joseph A. Jungmann, *The Mass of the Roman Rite: Its Origins and Development* (New York: Benziger Bros., 1959), 417.
25. Thomas Talley, "The Literary Structure of the Eucharistic Prayer," *Worship* 58:408.
26. "Holy, holy, holy is the LORD of hosts."
27. "Hear, O Israel: The LORD is our God, the LORD alone" (Deut. 6:4). However, Brian Spinks believes that it is more likely that "the Christian synagogue had adopted forms including Sanctus for morning prayer, such forms as we find in *Apostolic Constitutions* 7:35 and *Te Deum*, and that it was from such Christian usage rather than directly from the synagogue in Judaism that such a praise of the Creator ending in Sanctus entered the anaphoral tradition" ("The Jewish Sources for the Sanctus," *Heythrop Journal* 21 [1980]: 173).
28. "Blessed is the one who comes in the name of the LORD."
29. Spinks, "Jewish Sources," 419: "From Cappadocia to Edessa by circa 300, the eucharistic prayer celebrated in a Christian form the 'triad' of . . . the beginning of sacred history in Creation, the critical midpoint of that history in the Revelation of God in Christ and his inauguration of Redemption, and the future of the Covenant people moved by the indwelling of the Spirit toward the consummation of sacred history when that Redemption will be fulfilled—all of that the liturgical backdrop against which theological reflection completed the articulation of our trinitarian faith."
30. Ibid.
31. "Perhaps he introduced the Lord's Prayer so that it might model Christ's manner of praying as closely as possible" (Bradshaw, *Essays*, 148). For an adaptation of the eucharistic prayer from the Alexandrine Liturgy of St. Basil, see Great Thanksgiving F, *Book of Common Worship* (Louisville, KY: Westminster/John Knox Press, 1993), 146.

Chapter Two: Eucharistic Prayer in the Roman Tradition

1. R. C. J. Jasper and G. J. Cuming, *Prayers of the Eucharist: Early and Reformed*, 3rd ed. (Collegeville, MN: Liturgical Press, 1987), 31.

2. "We render thanks to you, O God, through your beloved child Jesus Christ, whom in the last times you sent to us as a savior and redeemer and angel of your will; who is your inseparable Word, through whom you made all things, and in whom you were well pleased. You sent him from heaven into a virgin's womb; and conceived in the womb, he was made flesh and was manifested as your Son, being born of the Holy Spirit and the Virgin. Fulfilling your will and gaining for you a holy people, he stretched out his hands when he should suffer, that he might release from suffering those who have believed in you. And when he was betrayed to voluntary suffering that he might destroy death, and break the bonds of the devil, and tread down hell, and shine upon the righteous, and fix a term, and manifest the resurrection, he took bread and gave thanks to you, saying . . . , etc." (Jasper and Cuming, ibid., 35).
   A version of this prayer is included as Great Thanksgiving G in the *Book of Common Worship* (Louisville, KY: Westminster/John Knox Press, 1993), 150–51.

3. *The Roman Missal: The Sacramentary* (Collegeville, MN: Liturgical Press, 1985), 502. The Sacramentary contains the approved rites for Mass in English translation, prepared by the International Committee on English in the Liturgy.

4. The new Roman Catholic eucharistic prayers include, for the first time, an explicit Epiclesis, or prayer for the Holy Spirit. In fact, they modify the Antiochene pattern by including two epicletic prayers, one before the Words of Institution and one after. The first prays for the sanctification of the bread and wine, and the second for the blessing of the communicants.

5. The Gregorian Sacramentary has ten Proper Prefaces, and more than one hundred in its appendix. The Gelasian has fifty-four, and the Leonine has two hundred sixty-seven.

6. Enrico Mazza, *The Eucharistic Prayers of the Roman Rite* (New York: Pueblo Publishing Co., 1986), 41.

7. Louis Bouyer, *Eucharist: Theology and Spirituality of the Eucharistic Prayer* (Notre Dame, IN: University of Notre Dame Press, 1968), 367.

8. "It may be said that the priest had become so enshrouded in the silence of the Canon that in the eyes of the faithful he appeared to vanish within it." At the same time, the priest added to the official Canon his own private devotional prayers. "Nothing of the old liturgy was left intact, and it came to be considered merely as a support for a private devotion which was inspired from other sources" (Bouyer, ibid., 377).

9. The priest alone was active. "The faithful, viewing what he is performing, are like spectators looking on at a mystery-filled drama of our Lord's Way of the Cross" (Joseph A. Jungmann, *The Mass of the Roman Rite: Its Origins and Development* [New York: Benziger Brothers, 1959], 88). "Spread on this canvas, the new prayers express only a pathos of personal unworthiness, mingled with pity before the sufferings of the Savior" (Bouyer, *Eucharist*, 379).

10. English quotations of the Roman Canon come from Mazza, *Eucharistic Prayers*.

11. *The Catholic Sunday Missal and Simplified Prayerbook* (New York: P. J. Kennedy & Sons, 1956), 89.

12. Jungmann, *The Mass*, 415.

13. Mazza, *Eucharistic Prayers*, 50. The English is a literal translation of the post–Vatican II official Latin text. The Latin text cited here is from *The Catholic Sunday Missal*, 90.

14. "Regarding the meaning of the words *mysterium fidei*, there is absolutely no agreement. A distant parallel is to be found in the *Apostolic Constitutions*, where our Lord is made to say at the consecration of the bread: 'This is the mystery of the New Testament, take of it, eat, it is My Body'" (Jungmann, *The Mass*, 421).

15. For example, "We praise You, we bless You, we give thanks to You, and we pray to You, Lord our God," from *The Divine Liturgy of Saint John Chrysostom* (Brookline, MA: Holy Cross Orthodox Press, 1985), 22. The same acclamation appears in the Liturgy of St. Basil; e.g., *The Liturgikon: The Book of Divine Services for the Priest and Deacon* (New York: Athens Printing Co., 1989), 291. *Apostolic Constitutions*, Book VIII, follows the institution narrative with these words, spoken by the presider: "Remembering then his Passion and death and resurrection from the dead, his return to heaven and his future second coming . . ." (Jasper and Cuming, *Prayers*, 110). The Liturgy of Saint James includes an acclamation of the people after the *verba*: "Your death, Lord, we proclaim and your Resurrection we confess" (Jasper and Cuming, *Prayers*, 92).

16. Paul F. Bradshaw, ed., *Essays on Early Eucharistic Prayers* (Collegeville, MN: Liturgical Press, 1997), 201.

17. "I tell you that from now on I will not drink of the fruit of the vine until the kingdom of God comes" (Luke 22:18); and "for as often as you eat this bread and drink the cup, you proclaim the Lord's death until he comes" (1 Cor. 11:26).

18. ". . . that [we] may praise and glorify Thee through Thy [*Beloved*] Child Jesus Christ through whom glory and honour [*be*] unto Thee with (*the*) Holy Spirit in Thy holy Church now [*and for ever*] world without end. Amen" (Bard Thompson, *Liturgies of the Western Church* [Philadelphia: Fortress Press, 1961], 21).

19. Alan F. Detscher in Frank C. Senn, ed., *New Eucharistic Prayers: An Ecumenical Study of Their Development and Structure* (New York/Mahwah: Paulist Press, 1987), 26.

20. Annibale Bugnini, *The Reform of the Liturgy 1948–1975* (Collegeville, MN: Liturgical Press, 1990), 448.

21. Ibid., 449.

22. Ibid., 451.

23. Ibid., 459.

24. E.g., The Liturgy of Saints Addai and Mari, the *Apostolic Constitutions*, and a number of others, probably including Justin Martyr's eucharistic prayer (ca. AD 150) (Robert E. Taft, "Mass without the Consecration? The Historic Agreement on the Eucharist between the Catholic Church and the Assyrian Church of the East Promulgated 26 October 2001," in *Worship* 77.6 [November 2003]: 490, 493). Also, Mazza, *Eucharistic Prayers*, 259. "We draw, then, the same conclusion for the account of institution as for the Epiclesis; it was not an original part of the anaphora, but once it appeared, it brought out so well the singleness of Christ's work and the dependence of our Eucharist on the 'once for all' of the Last Supper that it has become an irrevocable part of the eucharistic prayer."

25. Jean-Jacques von Allmen, *The Lord's Supper* (London: Lutterworth Press, n.d.), 33.

26. "In modern times no less an authority on the Roman Eucharist than the great Joseph A. Jungmann S.J. sums up the original tradition of the undivided church as follows: 'In general Christian antiquity, even until way into the Middle Ages,

manifested no particular interest regarding the determination of the precise moment of the consecration. Often reference was made merely to the entire eucharistic prayer' " (Taft, "Mass without Consecration?" 497).

27. Pius VII reiterated this point of view even more forcefully in a statement issued in 1822 (Taft, "Mass without Consecration?" 498–99).

28. "In Thomas's view, a valid consecration depends solely on the (explanatory) words of the Lord, without reference to the rest of the Canon. Henceforth, the Canon was regarded simply as a framework lending solemnity to the words of consecration" Mazza, *Eucharistic Prayers*, 261).

29. "Nowadays, the prevailing opinion, based on P. Cagin's study in comparative liturgy, is that the entire anaphora is the form of the eucharist" (Mazza, *Eucharistic Prayers*, 257). In the Orthodox church, the Epiclesis (invocation of the Holy Spirit) has traditionally been understood to effect the consecration. Fr. Alexander Schmemann (1921–83), an Orthodox theologian, argues forcefully that it is not only the Epiclesis, or the Words of Institution, or even the anaphora (the eucharistic prayer) as a whole that effects consecration, but that it is the entire *ordo* of the liturgy that has that function. No single piece of the liturgy can be lifted out as though it alone is important. "But from the standpoint of Tradition the sacramental character of the Eucharist cannot be artificially narrowed to one act, to one moment of the whole rite. We have an '*ordo*' in which all parts and all elements are essential, are organically linked together in one sacramental structure. In other words, the Eucharist is a sacrament from the beginning to the end and its fulfillment or consummation is 'made possible' by the entire liturgy" (*Liturgy and Tradition: Theological Reflections of Alexander Schmemann*, ed., Thomas Fisch [Crestwood, NY: St. Vladimir's Seminary Press, 2003], 82).

"The very ideas of a moment of consecration and also of the *essential* and *non-essential* acts in the liturgy, etc., are not adequate—should not be applied in Eucharistic theology" (Ibid., 104).

Chapter Three: Eucharistic Prayer and the Reformation

1. "But after Christ's sacrifice was accomplished, the Lord instituted another method for us, that is, to transmit to the believing folk the benefit of the sacrifice offered to himself by his Son. He has therefore given us a Table at which to feast, not an altar upon which to offer a victim" (John Calvin, *Institutes of the Christian Religion*, ed., John T. McNeill and Ford Lewis Battles [Philadelphia: Westminster Press, 1960], 4.18.12. [1440]).

2. *Service Book and Hymnal* (Minneapolis: Augsburg Publishing House, 1958), 34, 35.

3. *Lutheran Book of Worship* (Minneapolis: Augsburg Publishing House, 1978). The order for Holy Communion, Setting One, offers the option of a prayer that consists solely of opening dialogue, Preface, Sanctus, and Words of Institution (following older Lutheran tradition), or a complete, tripartite eucharistic prayer (69), as also do Setting Two (89) and Setting Three (110).

4. Bard Thompson, *Reformed Liturgies in Translation* (Theological Seminary of the Evangelical and Reformed Church, 1956, 1957), 15.

5. The Reformed removed the institution narrative from the prayer to be used either before or after it, because they understood the *verba* to have been addressed to the disciples rather than to God. God, of course, did not need to be reminded of the Last Supper or of Christ's death and resurrection (or, for

that matter, of the creation, sending of the prophets, etc.). On the other hand, one might consider whether the command to "do this in remembrance of me" might not be construed as a kind of remembering before God. For example, a child might remind a parent of a past incident in which the parent comforted and consoled the child with the promise that everything would be all right. The child may recall the event frequently, and the parent has not forgotten, yet the child invites the remembering as a kind of sharing of the past occasion and evokes it in solidarity with the parent as a common affirmation of the promises that accompanied it.

6. "So if you have been raised with Christ, seek the things that are above, where Christ is, seated at the right hand of God."

7. Thompson, *Reformed Liturgies*, 42.

8. Cf. Calvin with Orthodox theologian Alexander Schmemann (1921–83). Calvin says, "But if we are lifted up to heaven with our eyes and minds, to seek Christ there in the glory of his Kingdom, as the symbols invite us to him in his wholeness, so under the symbol of bread we shall be fed by his body, under the symbol of wine we shall separately drink his blood, to enjoy him at last in his wholeness. . . . This Kingdom is neither bounded by location in space nor circumscribed by any limits" (*Institutes*, 4.17.18 [1381]). Schmemann says, referring to the opening dialogue, "The next exclamation of the celebrant, 'Let us lift up our hearts,' we find in no other service—it belongs entirely and exclusively to the divine liturgy. For this exclamation is not simply a call to a certain lofty disposition. In the light of all that has been said above, it is an affirmation that the eucharist is accomplished not on earth but in heaven. . . . We can lift our hearts 'on high' because this 'on high,' this heaven is within us and among us, because it has been returned, restored to us as our real homeland of the heart's desire, to which we returned after an agonizing exile, for which we have always groaned with homesickness, and through the memory of which all creation lives" (*The Eucharist: Sacrament of the Kingdom* [Crestwood, NY: St. Vladimir's Seminary Press, 2000], 168). Also, in commenting on the mention of angels in the Preface leading to the Sanctus, Schmemann writes, "The liturgical function of this mention (and this also is true of the *Sanctus*) is to certify that the Church has entered its heavenly dimension, has *ascended into heaven*. It indicates that we are now at the throne of God, where the angels eternally sing 'Holy, Holy, Holy.'" And also, "For a long time the movement of the Liturgy was explained as a movement *downwards*: as grace which the priest takes 'from heaven' and brings down to us. It seems to me that such an explanation must be completed by its opposite. It is not God who is being taken from heaven, placed on our altars, and then put into the mouths of men. It is the Church that is being lifted up and ascends to heaven. A very important liturgical category is that of Christ's Ascension, and we must not forget that the first manual of liturgies, the Epistle to the Hebrews, was written precisely in terms of Ascension" (*Liturgy and Tradition: Theological Reflections of Alexander Schmemann*, ed., Thomas Fisch [Crestwood, NY: St. Vladimir's Seminary Press, 2003], 107–8).

9. "The Supper could have been administered most becomingly if it were set before the church very often, and at least once a week. First, then, it should begin with public prayers. After this a sermon should be given. Then, when bread and wine have been placed on the Table, the minister should repeat the words of institution of the Supper. Next, he should recite the promises which were left to us in it: at the same time, he should excommunicate all who are

debarred from it by the Lord's prohibition. Afterward, he should pray that the Lord, with the kindness wherewith he has bestowed this sacred food upon us, also teach and form us to receive it with faith and thankfulness of heart. . . . But here either psalms should be sung, or something be read, and in becoming order the believers should partake of the most holy banquet, the ministers breaking the bread and giving the cup. When the Supper is finished, there should be an exhortation to sincere faith and confession of faith, to love and behavior worthy of all Christians. At the last, thanks should be given, and praises sung to God. When these things are ended, the church should be dismissed in peace" (Calvin, *Institutes*, 4.17.43 [1421 and 1422]).

10. John Calvin, *The Form of Church Prayers and Hymns with the Manner of Administering the Sacraments and Consecrating Marriage According to the Custom of the Ancient Church*, in R. C. D. Jasper and G. J. Cuming, *Prayers of the Eucharist: Early and Reformed* (Collegeville, MN: Liturgical Press, 1990), 213.

11. John Calvin, *La Forme des Prières* (The Form of Church Prayers), Bard Thompson, *Liturgies of the Western Church* (Philadelphia: Fortress Press, 1961), 183.

12. Ibid., 159.

13. "We previously discussed how the Sacrament of the Sacred Supper serves our faith before God. But the Lord here not only recalls to our memory, as we have already explained, the abundance of his bounty, but, so to speak, gives it into our hand and arouses us to recognize it. At the same time he admonishes us not to be ungrateful for such lavish beneficence, but rather to proclaim it with fitting praises and to celebrate it with thanksgiving" (Calvin, *Institutes*, 4 17 37 [1414]).

14. The prayers after the sermon take the form of intercessions, for "rulers and governors," "the needs of thy people," and "all mankind." The prayer is offered for "all princes and lords," "the magistrates of this city," "ordained pastors," and "for all men everywhere." The prayer continues quite specifically for "those whom thou dost visit and chasten with cross and tribulation, whether by poverty, prison, sickness, or banishment, or any other misery of the body or affliction of the spirit." There is prayer that those gathered might "hear His [Jesus'] Word (and . . . keep His holy Supper.") It includes an eschatological reference, that "every power and principality which stands against thy glory be destroyed and abolished day by day, till the fulfillment of thy kingdom be manifest, when thou shalt appear in judgment." Continuing, there are petitions for the congregation, specifically that God might "strengthen us by thy Holy Spirit and arm us with thy grace" (Calvin, in Thompson, *Liturgies of the Western Church*, 199–202). For Communion Sundays, Calvin adds a prayer with explicit eucharistic reference. (See Appendix B.)

15. Thompson, *Liturgies of the Western Church*, 208.

16. Thompson, *Reformed Liturgies*, 8. In the Zurich Liturgy, the server says, "Dear brothers, in keeping with observance and institution of our Lord Jesus Christ, we now desire to *eat* the bread and drink the cup which He has commanded us to use in commemoration, praise and thanksgiving that He suffered death for us and shed His blood to wash away our sin" (Thompson, *Liturgies of the Western Church*, 153).

17. Calvin quoted "David" who, he said, called thanksgivings "the sacrifices of praise." "The Lord's Supper cannot be without a sacrifice of this kind, in which, while we proclaim his death [1 Cor. 11:26] and give thanks, we do nothing but offer a sacrifice of praise. From this office of sacrificing, all Christians are called

a royal priesthood [1 Peter 2:9], because through Christ we offer that sacrifice of praise to God of which the apostles speak: 'the fruit of lips confessing his name [Heb. 13:15, Vg]'" (Calvin, *Institutes*, 4.18.17 [1445]). Cf. with contemporary Orthodox theologian, Alexander Schmemann: "The first and real sacrifice is thus, the sacrifice of the Church itself. But (and this 'but' is very important) it is a *sacrifice in Christ*. It is not a new sacrifice because it is the sacrifice of the Church, and the Church is the Body of Christ. From the first moment of the Liturgy, Christ is not only the One who *accepts* the sacrifice, but in the words of one of the liturgical prayers, the One who also *offers*. All our sacrifices—and a Christian is by his very nature a living sacrifice to God—converge at the one and unique sacrifice, full and perfect, that of Christ's humanity, which He offered to God and in which we are included through our membership in the Church" (Schmemann, *Liturgy and Tradition*, 109).

18. Bryan D. Spinks, *From the Lord and 'The Best Reformed Churches': A Study of the Eucharistic Liturgy in the English Puritan and Separatist Traditions, 1550–1633* (Rome: Edizioni Liturgiche, 1984), 63.

19. Thompson, *Liturgies of the Western Church*, 207.

20. Hughes Oliphant Old, *The Patristic Roots of Reformed Worship* (Zurich: Theologischer Verlag, 1975).

21. "Now, that sacred partaking of his flesh and blood, by which Christ pours his life into us, as if it penetrated into our bones and marrow, he also testifies and seals in the Supper—not by presenting a vain and empty sign, but by manifesting there the effectiveness of his Spirit to fulfill what he promises" (Calvin *Institutes*, 4.47.11 [1373]). "If the Spirit be lacking, the sacraments can accomplish nothing more in our minds than the splendor of the sun shining upon blind eyes, or a voice sounding in deaf ears" (Ibid., 4.14.9 [1284]). "Yet a serious wrong is done to the Holy Spirit, unless we believe that it is through his incomprehensible power that we come to partake of Christ's flesh and blood" (Ibid., 4.17.33 [1405]). Cf. Schmemann, the Orthodox theologian: "And so, the liturgy is accomplished in the *new time* through the Holy Spirit. It is entirely, from beginning to end, an *epiklesis*, an invocation of the Holy Spirit, who transfigures everything done in it, each solemn rite, into that which it manifests and reveals to us." Some sort of sacramental "conversion" takes place, "but this conversion remains invisible, for it is accomplished by the Holy Spirit, in the new time, and is certified only by *faith*. So also the conversion of the bread and wine into the holy body and blood of Christ is accomplished invisibly. Nothing perceptible *happens*—the bread remains bread, and the wine remains wine. For if it occurred 'palpably,' then Christianity would be a magical cult and not a religion of faith, hope, and love" (Schmemann, *Eucharist*, 222).

22. *The Constitution of the Presbyterian Church (U.S.A.)*, Part I, *Book of Confessions* (Louisville, KY: Office of the General Assembly), 3.21. See also 5.196 and 4.079. The Second Helvetic Confession of 1561, the Heidelberg Catechism of 1562, and the French Confession of 1559 make the same affirmation.

23. "The question, which for a long time has been not only central but almost the only question in all Eucharistic theology—namely, *what* happens to the elements (and the *how* and the *when*)—must not precede, but must follow another basic question. *What happens to the Church in the Eucharist?* For it is only when this question is asked that certain of the affirmations made by the Eastern Church can be understood: the affirmation—for example, that the very ideas

of a moment of consecration and also of the *essential* and the *non-essential* acts in the liturgy, etc., are not adequate—should not be applied in Eucharist theology" (Schmemann, *Liturgy and Tradition*, 104).

24. Thurian says that Calvin derived his theology of the Holy Spirit in the Eucharist "from a sermon attributed to John Chrysostom by Erasmus and printed in the edition of his works published at Basel in 1530" (Max Thurian, *The Eucharistic Memorial*, Part II [Richmond: John Knox Press, 1961], 113).

25. Calvin, *Institutes*, 4.17.39 (1416).

26. Ibid.

27. Ibid.

28. *The Constitution of the Presbyterian Church (U.S.A.)*, Part I, *Book of Confessions* (Louisville, KY: Office of the General Assembly, 1996), 5.178 (101). Although not precisely parallel, at least one and probably several early eucharistic prayers include an Epiclesis of the *logos* (Word) rather than of the Holy Spirit. The anaphora ascribed to Sarapion of Thmuis includes, in a section of the prayer following the Words of Institution, the petition, "God of truth, let your holy Word come upon this bread, in order that the bread may become body of the Word, and upon this cup, in order that the cup may become blood of truth" (Maxwell E. Johnson, "The Archaic Nature of the Sanctus, Institution Narrative, and Epiclesis of the Logos in the Anaphora Ascribed to Sarapion of Thmuis," in Paul F. Bradshaw, ed., *Essays on Early Eastern Eucharistic Prayers* [Collegeville, MN: Liturgical Press, 1997], 86). This invocation of the *logos* understands "Word" differently than in the Reformed usage, which links the "Word" directly with preaching and/or the formulaic use of the Words of Institution, but there remains, nevertheless, an intriguing similarity.

29. *The Book of Common Order of the Church of Scotland: Commonly Known as John Knox's Liturgy* (Edinburgh and London: William Blackwood & Sons, 1901), 124.

30. "And these most inestimable benefits we acknowledge and confess to have received of Thy free mercy and grace, by Thine only beloved Son Jesus Christ, for the which therefore, we Thy congregation, moved by Thy Holy Spirit, render Thee all thanks, praise, and glory, for ever and ever. Amen" (Ibid., 125).

31. W. D. Maxwell, *An Outline of Christian Worship: Its Development and Forms* (London: Oxford University Press, 1960), 125. "Caldewood, writing about 1620, says that it had been the custom in Scotland for sixty years, that is, since the first days of the Reformation, to 'bless' the Bread and Wine" (John M. Barkley, *Worship of the Reformed Churches* [Richmond: John Knox Press, 1967], 50). Also, Forrester declares that the 1637 Book of Common Prayer, commissioned by Charles I for use in Scotland, "was by no means devoid of concessions to existing Scottish practice and tradition, such as . . . the inclusion of an *epiclesis*, which the English book lacked" (Duncan Forrester and Douglas Murray, eds., *Studies in the History of Worship in Scotland* [Edinburgh: T & T Clark, 1984], 48).

32. Thompson, *Liturgies of the Western Church*, 257. E. C. Ratcliff suggests that, by invoking both the Word and the Spirit, the 1549 Epiclesis "gives liturgical expression to a well-known Western doctrine which had descended to the sixteenth century from Paschasius Radbertus by way of Gratian's *Decretum*, and with which even English layfolk were acquainted through the Corpus Christi sermon in John Mirk's *Festywall*: the sermon refers to the sacraments as 'goddes owne body in fourme of breed made by the vertue of crystes wordes that

the preste sayth and by werkynge of ye holy gooste'" (E. C. Ratcliff, *Liturgical Studies*, ed., A. H. Couratin and D. H. Tripp [London: SPCK, 1976], 206).

33. Gordon Donaldson, *The Making of the Scottish Prayer Book of 1637* (Edinburgh: The University Press, 1954), 68.

34. Jungmann, Joseph A., *The Mass of the Roman Rite: Its Origins and Development* (New York: Benziger Brothers), 34–36, 58. Jungmann suggests that the Gallic rites may have originated in Milan. "Accordingly, if we suppose that one of Milan's bishops who came from the Orient—like the Cappadocian Auxentius (355–374)—had established this liturgical type, then we can explain many of the coincidences with oriental usage, more particularly with Antioch—coincidences which are features of the Gallican liturgies and distinguish them from the Roman" (*The Mass*, 35).

35. *The Book of Common Prayer and Administration of the Sacraments and Other Parts of Divine Service for the use of the Church of Scotland* (Commonly known as Laud's Liturgy [1637]) (Edinburgh and London: William Blackwood & Sons, 1904), 129. The American prayer book, adopted in 1789, has a nearly identical eucharistic prayer. The Epiclesis has only slightly different wording: "And we most humbly beseech thee, O merciful Father, to hear us; and, of thy almighty goodness, vouchsafe to bless and sanctify, with thy Word and Holy Spirit, these thy gifts and creatures of bread and wine" (*The Book of Common Prayer and Administration of the Sacraments and Other Rites and Ceremonies of the Church according to the Use of The Protestant Episcopal Church in the United States of America* [New York: Oxford/Henry Frowde, 1892], 236).

36. See n. 28.

37. *The Book of Common Prayer from The Original Manuscript attached to The Act of Uniformity of 1662* (London: Eyre & Spottiswoode, 1892), 251.

38. Jasper and Cuming, *Prayers of the Eucharist*, 260.

39. Ibid., 290, 291.

40. Ibid., 312.

41. Donaldson, *The Making of the Scottish Prayer Book*, n. 77. See also Jasper and Cuming, *Prayers of the Eucharist*, 258: "Nor would the permission to consecrate further supplies of bread and wine when necessary simply by the use of the Words of Institution meet with universal approval" [by the Scots]. For contemporary practice in the American Episcopal Church, see *The Book of Common Prayer and Administration of the Sacraments and Other Rites and Ceremonies of the Church* (New York: Church Hymnal Corporation and Seabury Press, 1979), 408. For contemporary practice in England, see *Common Worship: Services and Prayers for the Church of England* (London: Church House Publishing, 2000), 296. For the history of Supplementary Consecration, see Marion J. Hatchett, *Commentary on the American Prayer Book* (HarperSanFrancisco, 1995), 388–90.

42. William McMillan, *The Worship of the Scottish Reformed Church, 1550–1638* (Dunfermline, Edinburgh, London: Lassodie Press, 1931), 171.

43. Thompson, *Liturgies of the Western Church*, 369.

44. Thomas Leishman, *The Westminster Directory* (Edinburgh and London: William Blackwood & Sons, 1901), 49.

45. *A Directory for the Publike Worship of God throughout the three Kingdoms of Scotland, Ireland, and England with an Act of the Generall Assembly of the Kirk of Scotland, for establishing and observing this present Directory* (Edinburgh: Printed by Evan Taylor, Printer to the Kings most Excellent Majestie, 1645), 50, 51.

46. Bryan D. Spinks, *Freedom or Order? The Eucharistic Liturgy in English Congregationalism 1645–1980* (Allison Park, PA: Pickwick Publications, 1984), 55.
47. Spinks, *Freedom or Order?* 59, and Thompson, *Liturgies of the Western Church*, 393 ff.
48. Spinks, *Freedom or Order?* 81.
49. Bryan D. Spinks, "The Origins of the Antipathy to Set Liturgical Forms in the English-Speaking Reformed Tradition," in Lukas Vischer, ed., *Christian Worship in Reformed Churches Past and Present* (Grand Rapids: Wm. B. Eerdmans Publishing Co., 2003), 67.
50. Ibid.,78.
51. Maxwell, *An Outline of Christian Worship*, 134.
52. The Directory for the Worship of God, *The Constitution of the Presbyterian Church in the United States of America* (Philadelphia: Published for the Office of the General Assembly by the Board of Christian Education of the Presbyterian Church in the U.S.A., 1954 [copyright 1888]), 345 ff. The chapter "Of the Administration of the Lord's Supper" "has remained unchanged since its adoption in 1788."

Chapter Four: Reform of Eucharistic Prayer in Modern Times

1. John Fenwick and Bryan Spinks, *Worship in Transition: The Liturgical Movement in the Twentieth Century* (New York: Continuum, 1995).
2. Bruno Bürki, "Reformed Worship in Continental Europe since the Seventeenth Century," in Lukas Vischer, ed., *Christian Worship in Reformed Churches Past and Present* (Grand Rapids: Wm. B. Eerdmans Publishing Co., 2003), 38.
3. R. C. D. Jasper and G. J. Cuming, *Prayers of the Eucharist: Early and Reformed*, rev. ed. (Collegeville, MN: Liturgical Press, 1990), 285–88.
4. James Hastings Nichols, ed., *The Mercersburg Theology* (New York: Oxford University Press, 1966), 277.
5. Gregg Alan Mast, *The Eucharistic Service of the Catholic Apostolic Church and Its Influence on Reformed Liturgical Renewals of the Nineteenth Century* (Lanham, MD, and London: Scarecrow Press, 1999).
6. *The Liturgy and Other Divine Offices of The Church* (London: Strageways & Walden, n.d.).
7. "Look upon us, O God, and bless and sanctify this bread. In the Name of the Father, and of the Son, and of the Holy Ghost, we bless this bread [cup]; and we beseech Thee, heavenly Father, to send down Thy Holy Spirit, and make it unto us the Body [Blood] of Thy Son, Jesus Christ" (Ibid., 15).
8. Jack Martin Maxwell, *Worship and Reformed Theology: The Liturgical Lessons of Mercersburg* (Pittsburgh: Pickwick Press, 1976), 382.
9. Nichols, *Mercersburg Theology*.
10. Bürki, "Reformed Worship," 47.
11. Charles W. Shields, *The Book of Common Prayer and Administration of the Sacraments and Other Rites and Ceremonies of the Church as Amended by the Presbyterian Divines in the Royal Commission of 1661 and in Agreement with the Directory for Public Worship of The Presbyterian Church in the United States* (New York: Anson D. F. Randolph & Co., 1864).
12. Ibid., 244.
13. *Church Service Society Annual*, no. 35 (May 1965) (Cupar-Fife: J. & G. Innes, 1965), 4. "In 1863 a pamphlet on 'The Worship, Rites, and Ceremonies of the Church of Scotland' was published by the present writer, which contained the

following recommendation: 'There should be a self-constituted society of the liturgical scholars in the Church, who would, after due time and full consideration of the whole subject, draw up a Book of Prayer for Public Worship, and of forms for the administration of the sacraments and other special subjects, as a guide to the clergy. Antiquity, the Reformation, and our present practice should be all kept in view by their compilers. . . . The basis of this book should be the old Reformed Liturgy, but in the Greek and other Liturgies there are many golden sentences . . . which should also be incorporated with it.' On the 31st of January 1865, the Church Service Society was formed by a few young clergymen" (George W. Sprott, *Euchologion: A Book of Common Order being Forms of Prayer and administration of the Sacraments and other Ordinances of the Church*, Church Service Society [Edinburgh and London: William Blackwood & Sons, 1905 {first edition 1867}], xvii and xviii).

14. George W. Sprott, *Euchologion.*

15. "G. W. Sprott, a member of the editorial committee, reiterated the fact fifteen years later that the Euchologion was drawn from many sources but then observed, 'but it is based ultimately upon the Eastern Liturgies, like the American (German) Reformed, and Catholic Apostolic Services, from which it is largely borrowed'" (Mast, *Eucharistic Service*, 99).

16. George W. Sprott, *The Worship and Offices of the Church of Scotland* (Edinburgh and London: Wm. Blackwood & Sons, 1882), 119, 121.

17. The Epiclesis in *Euchologion* is "And we most humbly beseech Thee, O merciful Father, to vouchsafe unto us Thy gracious presence, and so to sanctify with Thy Word and Spirit these Thine own gifts of bread and wine which we set before Thee, that the bread which we break may be to us the communion of the body of Christ, and the cup of blessing which we bless the communion of the blood of Christ" (Sprott, *Euchologion*, 296–97).

18. William D. Maxwell, *A History of Worship in the Church of Scotland* (New York: Oxford University Press, 1955), 177.

19. William D. Maxwell, *An Outline of Christian Worship: Its Development and Forms* (London: Oxford University Press, 1960), 134.

20. "From the *Liturgy of the Catholic Apostolic Church*, through the *Euchologion* of Scotland, the words of a traditional Eucharistic prayer returned to the Dutch Reformed Church" (Mast, *Eucharistic Service*, 130).

21. *The Book of Common Worship, Published by Authority of the General Assembly of the Presbyterian Church in the United States of America* (Philadelphia: Presbyterian Board of Publication and Sabbath-School Work, 1906).

22. "Dearly beloved in the Lord, forasmuch as we be now assembled to celebrate the Holy Communion of the body and blood of our Saviour Christ" (George W. Sprott, *The Book of Common Order of the Church of Scotland: Commonly Known as John Knox's Liturgy* [Edinburgh and London: William Blackwood & Sons, 1901], 121).
Cf. *The Book of Common Prayer*, viz., "Dearly beloved in the Lord, ye who mind to come to the holy Communion of the Body and Blood of our Saviour Christ" (*The Book of Common Prayer and Administration of the Sacraments and other Rites and Ceremonies of the Church according to the use of the Protestant Episcopal Church in the United States of America* [New York: Henry Frowde, 1897], 229).

23. *Book of Common Worship*, revised, Approved by the General Assembly of the Presbyterian Church in the United States (Richmond: Presbyterian Committee of Publication, 1932).

24. Bürki, "Reformed Worship," 49.
25. *Book of Common Order* (London, Glasgow, Melbourne: Oxford University Press, 1940).
26. *The Book of Common Worship* (Philadelphia: Published for the Office of the General Assembly by the Publication Division of the Board of Christian Education of the Presbyterian Church in the United States of America, 1946). While the 1906 book adds the inscription, "For Voluntary Use in the Churches," the 1946 version reads, "Approved by the General Assembly of the Presbyterian Church in the United States of America."

Chapter Five: A Crescendo of Consensus

1. Bruno Bürki, "Reformed Worship in Continental Europe since the Seventeenth Century," in Lukas Vischer, ed., *Christian Worship in Reformed Churches Past and Present* (Grand Rapids: Wm. B. Eerdmans Publishing Co., 2003), 51.
2. Karl Barth, *The Preaching of the Gospel* (Philadelphia: Westminster Press, 1963), 23.
3. Bürki, "Reformed Worship," 54.
4. Directory for the Worship and Work of the Church, *The Book of Church Order* (Atlanta: The Office of the Stated Clerk of the General Assembly—The Presbyterian Church in the United States, 1963), 211–18.
5. *The Constitution of the United Presbyterian Church in the United States of America, Part II, Book of Order* (New York: Office of the General Assembly of the United Presbyterian Church in the United States of America, 1967), 21.031.
6. T. S. Garrett, *Worship in the Church of South India* (Richmond: John Knox Press, 1958), 9. An example is the St. James anaphora's reference to Christ as God's agent in creation and redemption:

Liturgy of Saint James	*CSI Liturgy*
Holy too is your only-begotten Son, our Lord	Through Jesus Christ thy Son our Lord, through
Jesus Christ, through whom you made all things . . .	whom thou didst create the heavens and the earth and all that in them is . . .

7. *The Book of Common Worship: As authorized by the Synod 1962* (London: Oxford University Press, 1963), 15. A note declares, "The material in this book was first published in a series of separate booklets in the years 1950–1962."
8. Ibid., 16.
9. "We hymn thee, we bless thee, we give thanks unto thee, O Lord, and we pray unto thee, O our God."
10. *Book of Common Worship*, 16, 17.
11. *The Worshipbook: Services* (Philadelphia: Westminster Press, 1970).
12. Ibid., 36.
13. *The Book of Common Order* (Edinburgh: Saint Andrew Press, 1979).
14. *Book of Common Order of the Church of Scotland* (Edinburgh: Saint Andrew Press, 1994). On p. 143, the 1994 *BCO* includes the following note: "The narrative of the Institution . . . may be incorporated within the Thanksgiving . . . thus: '. . . we follow his example and obey his command, who on the night of his arrest, took bread, etc.'"
15. Ibid., 129.
16. *A Book of Services: The United Reformed Church in England and Wales* (Edinburgh: Saint Andrew Press, 1980), 14.

17. *Liturgie: Herausgegeben im Auftrag der Liturgiekonferenz der Evangelisch-Reformierten Kirchen in der Deutschsprachigen Schweiz*, vol. 3, Abendmahl (Bern: Verlag Stämpfli & Cie AG, 1983).

18. *Liturgie: Herausgegeben im Auftrag der Liturgiekonferenz der Evangelisch-Reformierten Kirchen in der Deutschsprachigen Schweiz*, Gemeindeheft (Bern: Verlag Stämpfli & Cie AG, 1983).

19. *Baptism, Eucharist and Ministry* (Geneva: World Council of Churches Faith and Order Paper no. 111, 1982), ix.

20. Ibid, 10.

21. Ibid., 13.

22. "There is an intrinsic relationship between the words of institution, Christ's promise, and the *epiklesis*, the invocation of the Spirit, in the liturgy. The *epiklesis* in relation to the words of institution is located differently in various liturgical traditions. In the early liturgies the whole 'prayer action' was thought of as bringing about the reality promised by Christ. The invocation of the Spirit was made both on the community and on the elements of bread and wine. Recovery of such an understanding may help us overcome our difficulties concerning a special moment of consecration" (Ibid.).

23. *Liturgie du dimanche pour le temps ordinaire à l'usage des Églises réformées de la Suisse romande*, referenced in Bruno Bürki, "The Celebration of the Eucharist in *Common Order* and in the Continental Reformed Liturgies," in Bryan D. Spinks and Iain R. Torrance, eds., *To Glorify God: Essays on Modern Reformed Liturgy* (Grand Rapids: Wm B. Eerdmans Publishing Co., 1999), 230.

24. *Book of Worship: United Church of Christ* (New York: United Church of Christ Office for Church Life and Leadership, 1986).

25. *The Constitution of the Presbyterian Church (U.S.A.)*, Part II, *Book of Order* (Louisville, KY: Office of the General Assembly, 1998), W-3.3613.

26. *Book of Common Worship* (Louisville, KY: Westminster/John Knox Press, 1993), 69 ff.

27. The Agnus Dei is used instead as one optional response, along with the Kyrie and Trisagion, after the Prayer of Confession.

28. *Holy Is the Lord: Music for Lord's Day Worship* (Louisville, KY: Geneva Press, 2003).

29. *Common Worship: Services and Prayers for the Church of England* (London: Church House Publishing, 2000).

30. The first is, ". . . grant that by the power of your Holy Spirit these gifts of bread and wine may be to us his body and his blood" (Ibid., 185), and the second is, ". . . in the presence of your divine majesty, renew us by your Spirit" (Ibid., 187).

31. Prayer C: ". . . and grant that, by the power of your Holy Spirit, we receiving these gifts of your creation, this bread and this wine, according to your Son our Saviour Jesus Christ's holy institution, in remembrance of his death and passion, may be partakers of his most blessed body and blood" (Ibid., 192).

32. Ibid., 195. Prayer D.

33. *Liturgie de l'Église réformée de France* (Paris, 1996).

34. "Célébrées aux origines de l'Eglise dans le cadre de ce repas du soir, la fraction du pain et l'action de grâces pour la coupe constituent l'élément essentiel de ce rituel enraciné dans la tradition juive" (Ibid., 11).

35. *Dienstboek: een proeve* (Zoetermeer: Uitgeverij Boekencentrum, 1998).

36. *Reformierte Liturgie: Gebete und Ordnungen für die unter dem Wort versammelte*

Gemeinde (Wuppertal: Foedus-Verlag/Neukirchen-Vluyn: Neukirchener Verlag, 1999).

37. *Celebrate God's Presence: A Book of Services for The United Church of Canada* (Etobicoke, ON: United Church of Canada, 2000), 239.
38. Ibid., 244.
39. Ibid., 267.
40. *The United Methodist Book of Worship* (Nashville: United Methodist Publishing House, 1992).
41. *Lutheran Book of Worship* (Minneapolis: Augsburg Publishing House, 1978).
42. *The Book of Common Prayer and Administration of the Sacraments and Other Rites and Ceremonies of the Church* (New York: Church Hymnal Corporation and Seabury Press, 1979).
43. Ibid., 335.
44. Ibid., 363.
45. Reformed Church in America, "Order of Worship: The Lord's Day," http://www.rca.org/images/worship/liturgies/orderworship.pdf.
46. *Psalter Hymnal* (Grand Rapids: CRC Publications, 1987), 973.
47. Christian Reformed Church in North America, "The Lord's Supper 1994," http://www.crcna.org/whatweoffer/resources/synodical/liturgy/supper.asp.
48. "Lift Up Your Hearts unto the Lord" (#309) or "Lift Your Heart to the Lord" (#515), *Psalter Hymnal* (Grand Rapids: CRC Publications, 1987).
49. Bürki, "Celebration of the Eucharist in *Common Order*," 237.
50. Ibid., 237, 238. "The Eucharistic prayer with thanksgiving, *anamnesis* and *epiclesis* will in the future be an indispensable part of the Eucharistic celebration in the Reformed churches as well [as others]. This makes the celebration of the Lord's Supper a Eucharist as the Lord instituted it, with links to the berakah of the worship tradition of Judaism" (Bürki, "The Renewal of Worship in the Reformed Churches," *Reformed Liturgy & Music*, Special Issue, 1995. 6, 7).
51. *Book of Common Worship*, Korean Edition (Seoul: Publishing House, Presbyterian Church of Korea, 2001).

Chapter Six: Eucharistic Prayer Ecumenical and Reformed

1. *Book of Common Worship* (Louisville, KY: Westminster/John Knox Press, 1993), 69. This Great Thanksgiving was prepared for the *BCW* by Marney Ault Wasserman, according to Harold M. Daniels, *To God Alone Be Glory: The Story and Sources of the Book of Common Worship* (Louisville, KY: Geneva Press, 2003), 180.
2. See Geoffrey Wainwright, *Eucharist and Eschatology* (New York: Oxford University Press, 1981).
3. John M. Barkley, *Worship of the Reformed Churches* (Richmond: John Knox Press, 1967), 68.

Glossary of Terms

Agnus Dei. Latin. Literally, "Lamb of God."

Anamnesis. Greek. Remembrance, memory, memorial.

anaphora. Literally, "offering," originating in the Eastern church to refer to the eucharistic prayer. Equivalent to the Canon in the Roman Church, or Great Thanksgiving in recent Presbyterian usage.

Antiochene. Referring to a form of eucharistic prayer associated with the ancient see of Antioch.

Benedictus. Latin. Literally, "Blessed." Referring to the sung acclamation, "Blessed be he who comes in the name of the Lord."

berakah. Hebrew. Blessing.

Canon. Roman Catholic name for the eucharistic prayer, anaphora, or Great Thanksgiving.

embolism. Material added to a fixed liturgical text.

Epiclesis. Greek. Invocation of the Holy Spirit.

exhortation. In Reformed and some Anglican liturgies, part of the eucharistic service preceding the eucharistic prayer, to prepare the congregation for communion.

fraction. The breaking of the bread.

Great Amen. The people's "Amen" following the Trinitarian doxology at the close of the eucharistic prayer.

Great Thanksgiving. In Presbyterian usage, the anaphora or the Canon—the eucharistic prayer.

haggadah. Hebrew. The text of the liturgy used at the Passover Seder.

institution narrative. Words of Institution for the Lord's Supper, that is, 1 Corinthians 11:23–26; Matthew 26:26–29; Mark 14:22–25; Luke 22:19–20.

manual acts. The breaking of the bread and lifting or pouring of the cup.

Memorial Acclamation. People's sung response after the institution narrative, for example, "Christ has died, Christ is risen, Christ will come again."

oblation. Self-offering.

opening dialogue. Traditional introduction to eucharistic prayer, beginning with some variation on "The Lord be with you," and continuing in a responsive structure between the presider and the people.

ordo. Order, or structure of a liturgy.

peace. A liturgical exchange of words and/or gestures of reconciliation, originally the "holy kiss." See Romans 16:16.

prayer of humble access. Anglican. "We do not presume to come to this Thy Table . . ."

presider. The person whose responsibility it is to preside in the service; the person who offers the eucharistic prayer.

Sanctus. Latin. "Holy," referring to the people's song from Isaiah 6.

Shema. Hebrew. "Hear," as in the Jewish liturgy. "Hear, O Israel, the Lord is our God, the Lord alone." See Deuteronomy 6:4.

Sursum Corda. Latin. "Lift up your hearts."

transubstantiation. The transformation of bread and wine into the body and blood of Christ.

verba. Latin. Literally, "words," referring to the Words of Institution.

warrant. Authority, as in authority for celebrating the Lord's Supper.

Words of Institution. See "institution narrative" above.

Selected Bibliography

Barkley, John M. *Worship of the Reformed Churches*. Richmond: John Knox Press, 1967.
Barth, Karl. *The Preaching of the Gospel*. Philadelphia: Westminster Press, 1963.
Bouyer, Louis. *Eucharist: Theology and Spirituality of the Eucharistic Prayer*. Notre Dame, IN: University of Notre Dame Press, 1968.
Bradshaw, Paul, ed. *Essays on Early Eastern Eucharistic Prayers*. Collegeville, MN: Liturgical Press, 1997.
Bugnini, Annibale. *The Reform of the Liturgy 1948–1975*. Collegeville, MN: Liturgical Press, 1990.
Bürki, Bruno. "The Renewal of Worship in the Reformed Churches," *Reformed Liturgy and Music*, Special Issue, 1995.
Calvin, John. *Institutes of the Christian Religion*. Ed. John T. McNeill and Ford Lewis Battles. Philadelphia: Westminster Press, 1960.
Daniels, Harold M. *To God Alone Be Glory: The Story and Sources of the* Book of Common Worship. Louisville, KY: Geneva Press, 2003.
Donaldson, Gordon. *The Making of the Scottish Prayer Book of 1637*. Edinburgh: University Press, 1954.
Fenwick, John, and Bryan D. Spinks. *Worship in Transition: The Liturgical Movement in the Twentieth Century*. New York: Continuum, 1995.
Fitzgerald, J., trans. *Teaching of the Twelve Apostles*. New York: John B. Alden, 1891.
Forrester, Duncan, and Douglas Murray, eds. *Studies in the History of Worship in Scotland*. Edinburgh: T. & T. Clark, 1984.
Garrett, T. S. *Worship in the Church of South India*. Richmond: John Knox Press, 1958.
Gerrish, B. A. *Grace and Gratitude: The Eucharistic Theology of John Calvin*. Minneapolis: Fortress Press, 1993.
Hatchett, Marion J. *Commentary on the American Prayer Book*. San Francisco: HarperSanFrancisco, 1995.
Jasper, R. C. D., and G. J. Cuming. *Prayers of the Eucharist: Early and Reformed*. Collegeville, MN: Liturgical Press, 1990.
Jungmann, Joseph A. *The Mass of the Roman Rite: Its Origins and Development*. New York: Benziger Bros., 1959.

Leishman, Thomas. *The Westminster Directory*. Edinburgh and London: William Blackwood & Sons, 1901.

Mast, Gregg Alan. *The Eucharistic Service of the Catholic Apostolic Church and Its Influence on Reformed Liturgical Renewals of the Nineteenth Century*. Lanham, MD: Scarecrow Press, 1999.

Maxwell, W. D. *A History of Worship in the Church of Scotland*. New York: Oxford University Press, 1955.

———. *An Outline of Christian Worship: Its Development and Forms*. London: Oxford University Press, 1960.

Maxwell, Jack Martin. *Worship and Reformed Theology: The Liturgical Lessons of Mercersburg*. Pittsburgh: Pickwick Press, 1976.

Mazza, Enrico. *The Eucharistic Prayers of the Roman Rite*. New York: Pueblo Publishing Co., 1986.

McMillan, William. *The Worship of the Scottish Reformed Church, 1550–1638*. Dunfermline: Lassodie Press, 1931.

Nichols, James Hastings, ed. *The Mercersburg Theology*. New York: Oxford University Press, 1966.

Old, Hughes Oliphant. *The Patristic Roots of Reformed Worship*. Zurich: Theologischer Verlag, 1975.

Schmemann, Alexander. *The Eucharist: Sacrament of the Kingdom*. Crestwood, NY: St. Vladimir's Seminary Press, 2000.

———. *Liturgy and Tradition: Theological Reflections of Alexander Schmemann*. Ed. Thomas Fisch. Crestwood, NY: St. Vladimir's Seminary Press, 2003.

Senn, Frank C. *Christian Liturgy: Catholic and Evangelical*. Minneapolis: Fortress Press, 1997.

———, ed. *New Eucharistic Prayers: An Ecumenical Study of Their Development and Structure*. New York: Paulist Press, 1987.

Spinks, Bryan D. "Beware the Liturgical Horses! An English Interjection on Anaphoral Evolution." *Worship* 59 (May 1985).

———. *Freedom or Order? The Eucharistic Liturgy in English Congregationalism 1645–1980*. Allison Park, PA: Pickwick Publications, 1984.

———. *From the Lord and 'The Best Reformed Churches': A Study of the Eucharistic Liturgy in the English Puritan and Separatist Traditions, 1550–1663*. Rome: Edizioni Liturgiche, 1984.

———. "The Jewish Sources for the Sanctus." *The Heythrop Journal* 21 (1980).

Spinks, Bryan D., and Iain R. Torrance, eds. *To Glorify God: Essays on Modern Reformed Liturgy*. Grand Rapids: Wm. B. Eerdmans Publishing Co., 1999.

Sprott, George W. *Euchologion: A Book of Common Order Being Forms of Prayer and Administration of the Sacraments and Other Ordinances of the Church*. Edinburgh and London: William Blackwood & Sons, 1905.

———. *The Worship and Offices of the Church of Scotland*. Edinburgh and London: Wm. Blackwood & Sons, 1882.

Taft, Robert E. "Mass without the Consecration? The Historic Agreement on the Eucharist between the Catholic Church and the Assyrian Church of the East Promulgated 26 October 2001." *Worship* 77.6 (November 2003).

Talley, Thomas. "From Berakah to Eucharistia." *Worship* 50.

———. "The Literary Structure of the Eucharistic Prayer." *Worship* 58.

Thompson, Bard. *Liturgies of the Western Church*. Philadelphia: Fortress Press, 1961.

———. *Reformed Liturgies in Translation*. Theological Seminary of the Evangelical and Reformed Church, 1956, 1957.

Thurian, Max. *The Eucharistic Memorial, Part II.* Richmond: John Knox Press, 1961.
Vischer, Lukas, ed. *Christian Worship in Reformed Churches Past and Present.* Grand Rapids: Wm. B. Eerdmans Publishing Co., 2003.
Von Allmen, Jean-Jacques. *The Lord's Supper.* London: Lutterworth Press, n.d.
Wainwright, Geoffrey. *Eucharist and Eschatology.* New York: Oxford University Press, 1981.
World Council of Churches. *Baptism, Eucharist and Ministry.* Geneva: World Council of Churches, 1982.

Index